DEAR MUM

GEMMA MILNER

To Ronnie, my son, who is now three. He has turned my world back around. He's a whirlwind, and I hope one day he will realise how he saved my life and helped me find joy again.

To Michael, my husband. You saw it all, and you're still here. I will be indebted to you just for being there, by my side, silent while I grieved my misfortune.

Dad, you had the natural instinct for knowing when I was drowning, and you grabbed my hand so my nose was just above the water.

Preface

This book started as a journal. It was my form of therapy; a way for me to process my inner thoughts in an attempt to put them in some kind of order.

I started to write two weeks after her death and as my pen kept hitting the pages of my leather journal that she'd bought for me, I found myself writing to her, and searching for answers that I would never receive.

As the year progresses, the roller coaster of emotions come and go, and come again. After the great shock and emptiness come the guilt, anger, and numbness. They flow around in circles, hitting me like a boxer knocking me off my feet over and over. The wonder if this will ever ease.

I turned this journal into a book in an attempt to help someone in a similar situation to this. I couldn't let her die for nothing. I needed her death to be for something. She would be proud of that.

Chapter One

*T*he moment of no return.

Two weeks ago, you died. On Tuesday, 25 July 2017 at 11.15 pm you decided to take your own life.

It's 2.57 am. I'm awakened by my phone ringing. It's John. he was your husband. What does he want me for at this time of the morning? It can only be something to do with you. I picked up the phone panicked. 'John, is everything ok?'

He cried out, 'No!'

'Is Mum ok?'

'No. She's been killed.'

I couldn't believe what I was hearing. As the blood left my face, I felt as though everything around me was crumbling away and I was just here sitting on my bed with the phone to my ear. My heart starts to pound as though it's going to explode out of my chest and I begin to shake. As I speak, I can't get my words out right. 'I don't believe it. It's a mistake,' I stutter down the phone to him. 'John, I'm coming over.'

Michael, my husband, sits up in bed next to me and puts the lamp on. I can tell by his face he knows something terrible has happened. I tell him the news and his face goes pale, his brow creates a deep burrow between his eyebrows, and he says absolutely nothing.

I grab my phone and I call my older sister, Hayley. The three of us were best friends. We told each other everything. I call her twice with no answer. I've got to get hold of her. She can't be peacefully asleep in bed while all of this turmoil is happening and she is oblivious. I call Paul, her husband. I dial twice and he finally answers with a concerned and slightly panicked voice.

'Gem, what's happened?'

I didn't know how I could say out loud that my mum had died. How could I tell my sister that Mum was gone? 'Paul, it's Mum. She's been killed. She's dead.' As the words escape me, I feel the shock hit me even more.

He is in disbelief and he passes the phone to Hayley. Her voice is panicked, 'Hello?'

I cry out, 'Mum's died!' and she wails her pain down the phone to me.

We chuck some clothes on and Michael drives us to your house. It's only five minutes down the road but it feels as though it's miles away. I'm creating stories over and over in my mind. What could have killed you at this time of night? If you had died from natural causes or had an accident, John would have said you had died and not that you were killed. The shock is intense and I don't know what to do with myself. I'm shaking and crying but I have no tears. I'm hysterical but my body seems calm, and yet I'm almost certain that it is all a mistake, somehow.

We arrive on your drive and my heart sinks further. I see that your car is gone. That means you went out, and that means this could all be true. My delusion is starting to unravel, and it's starting to look possible that you could have been killed. I wanted this to be a big mistake, something that we could come to laugh at in the weeks to come. I jump out of the van and Michael follows me. The door is unlocked and the lights are on.

We run in and John's daughter Justine is in the living room doorway. She grabs me with a hug, and I see John on the sofa in utter despair. I now know it's true. You're dead. Justine isn't usually at the house. John must have called her first. He wouldn't have known what to do, or even how to tell me and Hayley.

I find myself standing silently, watching John cry on the sofa while rubbing my face with my hands over and over. I swallow the large tennis-ball-sized lump that's in my throat, and I ask John, 'How?'

Justine answers for him. 'It was a train.'

The word train pierces me like a knife entering and twisting. The blurry moments pass and I slowly digest the situation and I ask more questions. 'Was she in the car?'

Justine's face saddens. 'No.'

You must have parked up and gone for a walk and got in the way of the train. Didn't you hear it coming? It's not like you to go out alone at night.

'Justine, did she do it on purpose?'

Her head drops. 'I think she did.'

The knife keeps on twisting and it's squeezing the life out of me.

So, you parked up in the car park and you walked to the crossing, and then you stepped out in front of the train, on purpose? That same car park we used to park in when you took us to the big play park as kids in the summer holidays, and the pedestrian crossing we used to cross when you took us on the summery walks by the river. The memories are flooding in but the happy memories have been stolen; they are now blurry and mixed up with the vision of seeing you walking out over the crossing and waiting there to end it.

Michael has left to pick up Hayley. She can't safely drive the twenty-minute journey on her own. Not after hearing this news. Paul has to stay home with Olivia and Harry. They are just seven and four, how will they absorb such news? Will they understand what death is? I am curled up on the chair I always sit on when I come over for dinner each week. I have got your blanket wrapped around me with my face tucked in. I feel utterly in disbelief. My body is starting to shut down. I'm sick and weak. I keep having to run to the bathroom as everything I have inside of me leaves my body.

Hayley and Michael arrive, and I run over to Hayley, and we hold each other while we both cry. She begins to ask John questions, and I shut down. I retreat back to the armchair to curl up under the blanket. Eventually, everything goes quiet. Each of us in our own little position, frozen with shock while our minds allow the information to sink in. I can't cope down here anymore in this silence. I'm going upstairs to lie down. I take myself up the two flights of stairs and arrive in your loft converted spare bedroom. I am sitting at the end of the bed. I feel such pain everywhere. I can't swallow and I can't breathe. I begin to hit the bed over and over and cry as though I will never stop.

I can't think straight. My world has instantly fallen apart.

Guilt, anger, and physical pain; my chest feels as though it's going to explode with loss, sadness, and shock. You were in such pain that you couldn't see any light. You felt no joy, and couldn't cope another day. You chose to leave us because you believed you couldn't go on anymore. Why was that?

The police have rung John to tell him they will come and see us at 10 am to give us details. I don't want to hear any of it. Time is passing so slowly and I'm just waiting. But what am I waiting for? I am lying around on the bed or I'm back downstairs on the chair in silence. I have nothing to say. I am unsettled and fidgety.

I need to message all of my clients to tell them I can't shoe their horses today. I send out a one-size-fits-all message and explain that there has been a family tragedy and I would be in touch. I message a couple of other farrier colleagues and ask them if they could cover any of my emergency work while I sort myself out. That is the thing about the farrier community, most of us have each other's back when things go wrong.

We find a note.

I love you all so very much.

Hayley, Gemma, John, Olivia, Harry, and Baby Jack.

My love always

Xxxxxxxxxxxxxxxxxxxxxxxxxxxxxxxxxxxxx

I stare at the words on the page. It's your writing but it's not as neat as it usually is. It's written in a pink pen. I need to find the pen. Feel it, hold it, and save it. It's one of the final things you touched. I read the names one by one and I see the name Baby Jack; my son, my baby boy who was born too soon just over one-

and-a-half years ago. The pain still feels raw, my heart is still broken from losing him and now my heart is shattered.

The note is written on the back of your hysterectomy letter folded up on the coffee table next to your old leather armchair. Was that a clue? Was the hysterectomy to blame? It was only five weeks ago. Were your hormones all out of balance, and a couple of glasses of prosecco made you feel bad; so bad that you didn't want to be here anymore?

The police have arrived. I'm leaving. I'm taking the dogs for a walk – the Shih Tzu Burty and the little mixed-breed Lilly. I harness them up, and we head off out the back door into the torrential rain. We walk and find a tree. We sit and I cry.

The dogs seem confused. They must be wondering where you are, and they must be wondering why we are sitting around in silence while each of us keeps bursting into tears. I ring Dad, over twenty years has separated you both. He knew you had died, Hayley must have told him, but he didn't know how.

'Gem, how?'

I'm trying to keep the lump in my throat out of the way so I can tell him, 'She jumped in front of a train,' but as the words come out, I burst into tears and so does he.

I'm back at your house, and the police are still here. I'm going in through the back door so I don't see them. I really can't take any more of the details. I feel cowardly but I can't do it.

I've unharnessed the dogs, and I take myself upstairs. I feel like a child hiding away up here while they are in there listening to what's next. Donna is John's other daughter. She must have come while I was out. She shouts up to me to tell me the police have left.

I bring myself downstairs to sit with everyone. I'm silent. I allow the hours to pass and I slowly ask a few questions. I listen to each piece of information and it takes my breath away.

Time is passing so slowly. It is now way past lunchtime and we haven't eaten a thing. We can't. I text a few friends to let them know what has happened. I send the texts, and I wait for the responses. I find myself hoping the response will sort it all out, and bring you back to me. I ask Emma to sort my two horses out. She is one of the horse girls who has become a close friend. We usually help each other out with our horses. Deano, my gorgeous friendly Irish horse who you loved, and the lovely young Lenny who has got me working hard trying to turn him into my dream event horse.

Michael and I head home for a change of clothes and some time out. It's around 4 pm now. There is a knock on the door. It's Emma. She's holding a vase with flowers. I open the door. She's silent. She hugs me and I cry into her shoulder. I leave her shoulder wet, and she blows me a kiss. She leaves the flowers in my hand. My head is down with streams of tears falling out of my eyes while I close the door.

Michael and I lie on our bed and try to make sense of it all, but we can't find any.

You were so loved by us all... how did you want to leave us? How can you leave the grandchildren and John?

You had a lovely cottage and garden you worked so hard on, just like the ones from the magazines you like to read. What couldn't you see?

All the unanswered questions are killing me.

You will never meet the grandchildren I'll give you. I will never get to give you a kiss, and I will never hear that infectious laugh you had. My mum, my inspiration, my best friend gone by choice.

I miss you so much that my body aches. It's dull, gaunt, and it feels so heavy.

The moments are passing and it all seems cloudy. I wander around the caravan not really doing anything. I take a seat on the sofa and sob. Michael is smoking on the porch. Meanwhile, a little bird flies in and looks at me and flies off. Was that you, Mum? I wonder if I'm losing my mind. How can you be a little bird? But I can't help but wonder if it is you.

We have been living in the caravan for a while now. Do you remember after Jack died? I lost a big client of almost 100 horses so money became tight for us and we decided to move out of the rented house and into the little old damp caravan to save money so we could own a house one day.

All the coming days are a blur. I'm between the caravan and your house. I'm spending time with the family. Hayley and John contacted them in the first few hours of that dreaded morning. Everyone is quiet and so sad. There are random outbursts of sobbing that come from us all, in turn. Olivia and Harry seem confused and keep asking for you. All I feel is pain, and I feel as though I'm floating around. I'm here but not really. Everything is so loud and fast, and everyone in the village is just wandering around and getting on with their days. It seems so strange because behind your closed wooden doors, down your tiny little street is horror and turmoil. Our worlds are all upside down and messed up.

A week has passed. Michael and I have come to visit the place where you died, at the crossing. It's dark and damp, and there isn't anyone around. We park in the car park and I wonder where you parked. Was it in the same spot as us?

We have left you flowers, Mum; your favourites, lilies. I wrap them around the lamppost, and hear a train coming. We look at each other and take a step back as the train rumbles past us. We almost collapse to the floor. The noise, the vibration, the wind that blows past us is all too much, and it makes me cry all over again. I imagine you there, and actually taking a step out in front of the train rather than backwards away from it.

Hayley and Paul have already been and left you some flowers. There is a card in them, and the words make the tears fall faster.

My card to you:

Mum,

I can't believe that you have left us.

Life will never be the same.

I forgive you and I love you always.

Xxxxxxxxxxxxxxxxx

I hope the sun is shining where ever you are. The truth is I don't forgive you, not yet.

John and Hayley have been busy sorting out your funeral and all the details. I just cannot bear it so, I take Olivia and Harry to the park and play with them.

Olivia has been crying a lot. She seems depressed, and anxiety seems to be brewing. She says things like, 'Mummy, don't leave me,' 'Mummy, what if you don't come and get me from school?', 'Mummy, what if you and daddy die? Who will look after me and Harry?'

She is asking for you a lot, Mum. She misses you. You were both so close, and she is lost without you. Harry is angry. He has started shouting more, throwing things, and he can't quite keep his temper under control. He has been getting frustrated over silly things and lashing out at Olivia for it. He's started wetting the bed too. He says things like, 'Nanna used to wear bags like that,' or 'Nanna used to take us to that park'. He remembers things but gets mad when he can't remember the things Olivia talks about.

I've been with Hayley every day. Our family come and go and they are heartbroken.

Hayley's holiday is approaching, and I feel terrified to be apart from her. She is the only one who feels exactly how I feel.

Michael and I move in with John to keep him company. It also gives me some comfort. I'm taking sleeping tablets to get me through the long and dark nights. They help but they make me hallucinate, and it frightens me. After taking them, I lie in bed. The beams, the hanging lights, and the walls all move. They sway and they become one. I feel dizzy, faint, and very weak. I try and keep my eyes closed but behind my eyelids, I still see blurry things moving. It's disorientating and confusing.

Monday is here. It's the first day on my own. I've done two trims on old ponies and a pair of fronts on my friend's horse. They were all left in the stables for me so I didn't have to see anyone. I've been gone from your house for about two hours. I'm weak and my head hurts. I have to take my time, and being with the horses is a therapy for me.

I arrive at the caravan and sit down on the sofa. The emotional build-up is bursting at the seams. I cry and cry for hours. I can't breathe. I don't know what to do with all of this grief. I'm overcome with grief and pain. I look through pictures of us all, and I'm reminded of the good times we've had. It's made me so sad.

I think I'll go for a walk with music on and my boys, Ralph and Toby, the two Jack Russells. Ralph is eleven now. Do you remember when Hayley, Paul, and I bought him for you as a tiny puppy for your birthday, and after three years, you finally caved and let me have him. Ralph and I always had a special bond, and he loved coming to work with me on all the farmyards, chasing rats and being free.

Toby, the five-year-old dope, has finally calmed down. You always said he was a handful and a bit of a pain, but you learnt to love him and he loved you too. He would always curl up on your knee, and you couldn't resist a Toby cuddle. We get in the van and drive down to the dreaded car park. We walk past the train line and over by the river. We walk, and I cry. I feel closer to you here. I don't like the thought of you wherever you are. I want you somewhere I can get to you. I feel as though I'm searching for you, and if I keep on walking, I'll find you at the crossing, and just before you step out, I jump and push you to the ground away from the train.

Did you know how much we all loved you?

Did you know how missed you would be?

You were only fifty-six. You had so much life left to enjoy.

Hayley and I have your jewellery. We know how much you loved it. You used to be so very sentimental. I'm not so much. Hayley is more so than me but still not as much as you.

I've started to look for clues around the house. I think I'm still looking for you, but the result always ends up the same; I can't find you.

We go through the motions of existing each day.

I get carried away with my emotions. I go back to that day in my head. I feel desperate to search and find you.

John went to bed at 10.30 pm. You stayed up longer and you went into the kitchen to get your hysterectomy letter. You wrote the note with the pink pen on the kitchen table. You folded the note and left it on the coffee table by your chair.

You got out the spare car key and left it on the mantelpiece. You went upstairs and got changed.

Which clothes did you wear?

Did you blow John a kiss goodbye?

Did you plan it or was it a last-minute decision?

You got in the car and drove off. You parked in the car park. *Which space did you pick?* You went through the gate.

How long were you there before you died?

What were you thinking about?

Were you crying?

Did you feel scared?

I texted you at 10.20 pm. I told you I loved you, and you replied straight back.

You jumped in front of the last train at 11.15 pm.

Why wasn't the train early that day? Why didn't you miss it?

You left your St Christopher next to your bed. You only ever got that out when you needed some guidance.

Did you think of us?

Were you thinking that you would be reunited with your mam and dad?

Wish I had been there to talk to you, and tell you how much we would all miss you.

When the train hit you, where did you land?

Did you die instantly?

The poor train driver.

My life will never be the same. It can't be, can it?

I've been for a ride on Lenny. We were trotting along the air base, and a pretty swallow was swooping around us. It was small and petite. It was dark in colour and very fast. I said, 'Mum, follow us to the end of the field.' When the words came out of my mouth, I felt as though I had lost my mind but, anyway, the swallow followed alongside of us as we cantered all the way to the end of the field. I felt as though you were riding with me. At the end of the field, I said to the swallow, 'Bye,' and it flew off with its two friends who seemed to have been waiting for it to come back. They left in the opposite direction.

Was that you... with your mam and dad?

It's been three weeks now, and there is still no date for the funeral. Your body has been at Queen's Medical Centre for all this time. Are you in a freezer, like in the movies? Is your body in one piece? I dread to think.

Chapter Two

I've written a letter for your funeral from me, Hayley, Olivia, and Harry.

Dear Mum, our best friend,

We have been struck by this blast of pain, guilt, anger, sadness, and loss. Our hearts broke into pieces the very moment we heard the worst news ever imaginable, and they can never be repaired without you.

They say that time will heal, but time will teach us to live around the pain that we will always feel. We know you would never have wanted us to suffer like this.

You were an incredibly kind and caring person. You loved us with all of your heart.

Life has been so good because you made us appreciate the little things. You always made us appreciate our family, and how life is too short.

Our lives now will always be incomplete. When we triumph, there will also be great sadness because you will miss it.

We will have to believe that you are up there looking down on us, watching all our lives carrying on, and you will be watching with your mam and dad who you missed so greatly. You will be holding Baby Jack tight, and having half a Strongbow at the pub with your mam, dad, Darren, Brian, and Lorraine.

You and John were like two peas from the same pod. There was so much love and laughter. When we'd stay, we could hear you both chatting and giggling away in the morning. Probably laughing about the fun from the night before.

We all shared great times together either away; in the sun playing with Olivia and Harry in the pool or the sea, or a night out laughing and dancing away in the old pubs in Nottingham.

When you and John were on holiday, we used to count the days until you were back, especially the time you went to Jamaica, which was almost three weeks. We've never been apart from you for that long; so this journey we have ahead of us, we can't imagine what a lifetime apart will be like.

You taught us to always be kind, and you would say, 'Only say what you would want others to say to you; otherwise, say nothing.'

And animals, you loved all kinds of animals, apart from snakes. You hated snakes. But again, you taught us to be kind to them all.

When Hayley and Paul had our beautiful Olivia and our lovely Harry, and when Gemma and Michael had our dear Baby Jack, you whispered the same words to us both. 'Now you know how much I love you.'

Our dear mum who we will love forever and always.

We forgive your decision, and we will live on in happiness in memory of you. Not a day will go by where we won't have you right here with us.

Hayley, Gemma, Olivia, and Harry

X X X X

We finally get a date for the funeral – 21 August 2017 at 3.30 pm.

Thirty-five years previously, on the exact same date, you married Dad. Does that mean something or is it a coincidence?

We have come to visit you. You're in a box; the mahogany coffin. It's locked shut. It's exactly where you shouldn't be. Me, Hayley, John, Olivia, and Harry; it's the first time we've been able to be near you since. We all go in together. It's cold in here. You're there, right in front of us in that bloody coffin. Your picture is on top of it. In that photo, you were so beautiful and fresh looking. You were well then.

They won't let us see your body. You must be so torn up. I want to give you a hug and cry into your chest like I would have if you were alive. You would have been hugging me back and stroking my hair. We stand and stare at the box. We don't know what to do or say. We are rigid, and it's quiet. Olivia and Harry don't know what to do. They don't understand. We each take a turn on our own with you. When it's my turn I stand and I look at your photo. I can't speak. I have so much to say to you but if I speak, I'll explode. My tears won't stop, and I can't let them see me like that. I stay with you in silence for a few minutes. I leave before the ball escapes my throat. It's Hayley's turn.

My twenty-ninth birthday is here, and your funeral is in four days' time. It's the first birthday without you. It's a tough day. Michael is having a day off work to be with me. We go out and do a few trims on a group of horses. It's a dark and rainy day. It's just how I feel inside.

After work, we put the TV on, but I can't help but search around the house again. I'm getting carried away looking for a letter or a card you pre-wrote for me. I find nothing. I calmly and quietly cry. I was never a crying sort of person; I was a little bit stoic in my emotions but you have made it so easy for me now.

Michael's mum is coming over. We are going out for a meal. Julia is a very calm and quiet character; extremely caring and kind. When Jack died, she was there for us, and I know she will be there for us again. She has been in close contact with me throughout all of this so far. I find her comforting, and I trust her. I've known her for eight years now.

She has arrived. She looks at me with a soft face and asks me if I'm ok. I confide in her because I'm scared. I'm scared of myself. I pour my heart out and tell her that your death has opened up a door for me, and I've been given an option for when things get too much for me. I can escape and kill myself just like you did. Her face soon turns into a frown and she looks shocked and scared and she tries to talk some sense into me. She does on the surface. I've been thinking a lot about killing myself; maybe the same way you did.

A couple of foggy days have passed, and your funeral is fast approaching. After much thought, I've decided that I will not kill myself. I would never be able to do that because my pain and despair will be passed on; it will be passed to those I love the most, and they will be left with this burden; my burden on top of theirs. How could I transfer my pain to them? I'd be free, at peace and I'd leave them, the people I love more than I love myself, in another mound of destruction. I couldn't do that and if you knew what devastation you would create, you would still be here.

I am pretending to be ok, getting up out of bed each day, and going to work. I've been laughing and joking like I feel no pain. Yet inside, I'm broken and I sob while I drive to the next job. I wonder how I'll ever be able to feel joy, optimism, positivity, and look forward to life without you. I don't feel as though I can. After deciding that I won't kill myself, I can't help but wish I would get a disease that will kill me, so I can be out of this pain and misery.

～

It's here, the day we've all been dreading. Another first; your funeral. It is a slow morning. John, Michael, and I have breakfast, we sit around your dining table and laugh about the daft things you used to do.

Family and close friends arrive at the house. We toast you; our mum, his wife, their friend, their mother-in-law, and their nana. We cry or hide our tears. I'm like stone. I'm cold, I'm gaunt, frail, and pale. The frown that hasn't left my face is like having a brick resting on my forehead all the time. It never leaves.

You have arrived at your house in the coffin surrounded by beautiful flowers and your all-time favourite, cheese and onion crisps.

I feel numb and pained as the ball in my throat isn't allowing me to swallow, cry, or breathe. I feel nothing but pain.

The drive to the crematorium is slow, I'm holding my head down because when I look out of the window, I see people getting on with their lives, carrying out their daily routines, and I'm finding it so hard to watch. My fingers just twist around each other, over and over.

We pull up outside the chapel, and I see our family. I see their pain. I see it all over their faces. Michael, Paul, Matt, and Nicky lift you out of the car, and Hayley collapses, almost hitting the ground. Family carry her arm in arm to her seat.

I look at the floor to prevent my tears. I hold Olivia's hand and we follow you down the altar.

Father Joe speaks, and it's all perfect. You would have been so proud of what Hayley and John have created.

Olivia read a poem she wrote. She was strong and so brave. I felt proud.

Dear Nana-with-Baby-Lilly,

You were amazing, and we loved you so much. You were our best friend.

You always took us out and spoilt us! You always made us laugh, and we will always love you and remember you forever.

It's hard to see you go.

Lots of love from Olivia and Harry

Xxxxxxxxxxxxxxxxxxxxxxxxxxxxxxxxxxxxxxxxx

PS Emma and John have cut Burty's hair.

Xxxxxxxxxxxxxx

Everyone claps for her after.

Bless her, she always called you Nanna-with-Baby-Lilly because, for as long as she can remember, you had Lilly as a puppy, and she has always called me Emma because when she was young, she couldn't pronounce Gemma.

We reach the end of the service. My tribute song comes on. It's Bette Midler singing *Wind Beneath my Wings*. I break, and I sob out loud. I collapse forward with my face into my knees, and my grief escapes my numb and broken body. I feel Michael put his arm around me, trying to comfort me, and I feel my dad rubbing my back from behind me. The song ends.

I dry my eyes. I rise, and I walk towards your coffin. I stare at the picture that is sitting on top. I plant my head on the coffin, and I kiss it over and over. I think this is my final goodbye. I leave the handwritten letter that I wrote for you in the neatest writing to be cremated with you. I leave and stand outside to greet everyone and thank them for coming. They pour out of the chapel. I realise how many people are here. There must be over 200 people.

We have a party planned to celebrate your wonderful life.

It's been 6 weeks now, and my emotions keep moving back and forth. I find myself at anger; an emotion I haven't fully felt yet. It's hit me hard, and I realise I haven't forgiven you. I hate you. It's come from nowhere, and it's knocked me off my feet. I feel sharp and bitter, and I've decided it's best if I have some time off work before I snap at someone. I need to try and look for some piece.

I realise that I hate you so much because I love you and the pain it brings; it's agony. You created this uncontrollable roller coaster, and I'm a total mess. I'm someone different.

The days and weeks are passing. Time is travelling fast, yet I still feel the same.

Is this normal?

Am I normal?

People keep asking me how you died; such a hard question to answer. I tell them, 'I can't talk about it right now'. They under-stand. But the truth is, I can talk about it but only to people who I trust. I couldn't determine my reaction in response to someone telling me that you're selfish. They don't have any right to have an opinion on your death because they couldn't feel your pain. So,

I spare myself from any judgement. I don't think it was your choice. I think you felt like you didn't have one.

Doctors have told us that you had been suicidal since March 2017, and just four months later you died. No cry for help, just gone. Doctors say you were a low risk. You even managed to hide your true thoughts from fully trained mental-health doctors and nurses. You must have asked for help and then decided you were ok, and you would figure it out on your own. You were a trooper; so strong, so brave but full of agony in your final four months of living. You are my inspiration to live and to do something in honour of you. Can I help someone to survive suicide?

Or someone to survive after someone has died from suicide?

I'm starting to think a lot about the meaning of life.

What is the point?

We love, we lose?

We can be happy and we can be sad.

Is it people?

Money?

Offspring?

Love?

I'm struggling. I don't know what the meaning of my life is...

I had just been starting to feel glimpses of happiness again after I'd lost Jack, up until you died by choice. This has slammed me back down to the ground; but if at all possible, the ground has cracked, and I'm even further down into the dirt. It's so hard, way harder than before, to climb back up and knock the dust off because this time the dust is thicker and deeper than before. It's not coming off. Maybe as the days, weeks, months pass, little particles of the dust will fall, and possibly, one day I'll start to feel a little lighter again.

At this moment I feel so pained – my head, my throat, my chest, and my heart.

Can you die from a broken heart?

I miss you so much. I'm so sad that I never got to say goodbye.

How long were you living in mental pain before you looked for help?

Did it all stem from the loss of Grandma all those years ago? You were only seventeen when she died. I have so many questions that have no answers.

You were so soft, quiet, and caring. Why didn't you let one of us know that you were struggling? We would have helped you.

I'm in shock tonight. It's been ten weeks, and still I find myself in utter disbelief. You must have found it very hard to leave us.

I close my eyes and I see you clear as day; like you're right there in front of me.

I wish I could have helped you. I would have given up my job to care for you, and to make sure you would fight through your thoughts. You still had so much life left.

You have got me questioning our whole lives together. I look at photos and I think, was that smile a fake one?

Were you actually happy at that moment?

Were you actually having a good day or were you pretending?

I pretend to be happy. If I didn't, I would push everyone away. Who would want to be around someone who is as sad as me?

Never in a million years would I have guessed my life, your life, would have turned out this way. We were close and had so many happy times, but I want more time with you. Do you remember when I used to get cross at you for doing too much? That was only to protect you because of your bad back; the chronic pain you lived with yet you still got on with stuff the best you could.

If there is life after death, I hope you're at peace, in a safe place, and I hope you have no regrets.

Chapter Three

*T*his journey is so hard.

Loving, missing, needing to speak to you, and knowing I will never ever get to see you again, hear you, link arms with you, kiss your cheek, see your smile, and ask you for advice. You're gone for good, forever, and never to be there sat in your arm chair on a morning, drinking milk and putting on your make up; or laughing so hard that you're crying; kissing Lilly and Burty, watching the dramas and horror movies, and seeing your name on my phone when you call or text me.

I have so many reasons to live, but losing you in this way, without a goodbye, has left me scared, and wondering if I can ever move on and be happy.

I feel as though I have a wound so deep that when it heals and becomes a scar, it may re-open.

Sometimes the grief hits me so hard, I feel as though I'm drowning, and everything hurts so bad that I want to end it all in that instant.

Hayley and I went to see a medium out of desperation, to find some answers. It was the one we went to years ago, remember, Mum? The lady in Newark. She told you that your mam was there.

It's quite expensive, and we can't afford it, but we go anyway. We have gone in together and she speaks to Hayley first. It feels intense. We are both shaky and nervous. She tells us you are here with us, and she tells us how you died. I couldn't believe what I was hearing but I believe her. I believe that you are here trying to communicate with us. She continued to tell us that you felt a burden, and that you don't want us to remember you for how you died. You want us to think that you're just gone. How can we though?

Is it real, Mum? Are you really able to talk to special people?

Can I be one of those people? I'd like to talk to you.

The last time I saw you, you seemed to be unsettled. You were disorientated, and you didn't look as smart as you usually did.

What was going on in your head? The next day you died.

We had lunch. I asked you if you wanted to come away on a big family holiday. You said, 'Yes, that would be lovely,' but you said it in a distant way, a bit like you were fobbing me off. I knew you weren't 100%, and I wanted to give you something to look forward to. You never drank in the day but you had two ciders and wanted to stay for another, but I had to go to sort the horses out. I wish I had stayed for that final drink.

After we left the pub and were in the car park, you almost walked off without giving me a hug goodbye. I grabbed you, hugged, you, and kissed your cheek, and told you that I loved you. If only I knew that would be the last hug, the last kiss, and the last time I would hear your voice. I was shocked that you forgot to say goodbye to me. You have never done anything like that before. Your mind must have been so confused.

There are some very bad days. I have to force myself to get up out of bed, and get on with my daily routine of work, my horses, and my dogs. On the outside, I look to have control, but on the inside, I'm sobbing. My whole life, leading up to this event, was starting to feel full of potential and hope, and now all there is, is this.

I feel damaged like I'll never be fixed.

I feel as though you and I were the same in many ways. It makes me feel as though I understood you, but it also fills me with fear. What if one day I lose myself in the same way that you lost your self?

When you used to watch your TV programmes, if they had sad parts in them, you would cry your heart out; but real things in your life, you would take yourself off and you would cry alone. I'm the same. I hate losing control, and I hate crying in front of anyone. I find it embarrassing, and I get mad at myself for doing it.

Looking back, did you cry enough? Should you have cried more to let out the pain? Is that how it works?

Since you've left, I've cried a lot. I didn't know I could cry so many tears but they keep coming and I can't stop them.

I can't help but panic at the thought of a lifetime without you. How can I do that?

You always laughed at the things that should upset you. Was that to cover up your pain?

But I'm the same. I laugh just as you did. But Mum, for you, I'm working on it. I'm getting the help I wish you'd had. Maybe then you'd still be here. I have started to see a therapist. His name is Kevin. Hayley and I both go together. We answer his questions, and it helps put our issues in order, a bit like a filing cabinet. We talk about each section of our grief. Once we understand it and have learnt to deal with the emotions of that section, we put it in a folder, into the filing cabinet, and shut it away in our minds. Sometimes we may want to open up that file and take a look at it but until then, it's nicely stored out of the way and we're ready to deal with the next section.

$\sim$

I wrote to you today.

My dear mum,

Words cannot express the loss I feel now that you are gone. I miss you so very much. My heart is broken. Until we meet again, my love.

You will be forever loved and missed every day.

Your little Gem Gem xxxx

Although I wish you hadn't taken your life from us, would that have been selfish of me? Would that have prolonged your agony if this wish had been granted?

How many times did you go to the railway line?

Each time you went down there, you were slowly and subconsciously getting your body and mind more used to the surroundings, the noises, and the trains. Then that final time you went there, you felt less scared, more comfortable with the situation, and it felt right?

Your agony has moved from you to us, I know this would have stopped you from jumping in front of that train, but how would you know that? Your twisted, confused mind wasn't thinking straight.

Chapter Four

We were out shopping about a year after Jack died. I saw a brown leather journal. It had leather strings wrapped around to seal it. 'I love this, Mum'.

You looked at me with a smile. 'Get it, Gem.' I thought about it while we wandered around the shop. I did think it would be lovely to fill it with the complicated emotions I had lingering around my mind after losing him. But I decided I shouldn't get it. Money was tight. I had been off work again for about a month because of the miscarriage.

That second baby was supposed to be our rainbow baby after Jack died; the baby that would help us get back on our feet, and feel love and joy again. That rainbow baby's heart stopped beating at eleven weeks and I carried it for thirteen. It was just seven months after losing Jack. It was quite a blow for us. I felt numb and it felt unfair. I was in a bad place but I just kept going. The stoic pattern I'd learnt from you; to pick your self back up, and push on forward.

It was Christmas. You gave me a present. I ripped open the wrapping paper, and it was a lovely brown leather bag. That made me smile.

'Gem, look in it.'

I looked at you with confusion, but I opened it up and there was that brown leather journal with the strings tightly wrapped around it. You were always so thoughtful like that. You never missed anyone's birthday, and you sent everyone a Christmas card every year. Even if you didn't see them much, they would receive a card in the post before Christmas Day.

I left my journal on the bedside table, waiting to fill it but I never managed to. I was starting to feel much more like me again, and I now wonder if that was because I couldn't bring myself to relive it all again? Ironically, now I fill it with the sorrow of your suicide.

We are now in October. It's been three months since your death. I'm in Yorkshire. I've booked a cottage on my own with the dogs. Michael and Hayley think it's a stint to kill myself so none of them will find me, but I reassure them that it's just for me. A chance for me to escape for a bit, listen to my music, write, walk in the countryside, and be in a place where no one knows what pain I am harbouring. Michael comes in his van for the weekend, and he leaves me Monday morning so he can get off to work. I look up at the ceiling in this tiny cottage and the beams look strong. They are perfect for someone to hang them self on, someone like me. I quickly look away and snap myself out of it. Imagine how Michael and Hayley would feel if I actually killed myself here when I promised them it was not my agenda.

Today, I feel so lost. I don't want to talk to anyone. I feel as though my life ended the night you ended yours.

It's a dark day with rain and wind. Today is a bad day.

This sharp acute pain that I feel everywhere, will it ever go away?

I have started to learn to meditate. I hope it will help me to control my thoughts. It's time to head home now, and I feel ready. I miss Michael so much. He seems to calm me. He levels out my anxiety, and makes sense of it all. He keeps me on a level that no one else can. He's a very calm character, and incredibly kind with a selfish streak at times. He's tall with dark hair and a short beard. He's handsome. He's ageing well. I do look at him at times and think to myself, how did I get so lucky?

I find myself cleaning, cleaning everything, just as you did. I used to rebel; I know how much that annoyed you. When I would meet you with creased clothes, you would say, 'I haven't brought you up to be so scruffy.' It used to make me laugh.

You were immaculate; your house, garden, car, and you; perfect for all to see. As I seem to be mimicking you, I find myself comforted from all this organisation.

If there is a place up there in heaven, does that mean you're with them, your mam and dad? I imagine you finally meeting them after all of those years apart.

I miss you. I hope you're with Jack.

What is he like?

Does he still have my nose?

And Michael's frown?

Do you grow in spirit or do you stay the same?

That dear baby Jack. I miss him. I had an operation to remove my endometriosis, and to ease my pain. It worked, and it also made a better chance for us to get pregnant, but we weren't quite ready for that yet. I was just twenty-five and Michael twenty-seven; business was good and busy, and we were very much making the most of it. We liked to go out drinking, and going away on holidays. The following year we got married in Las Vegas and we were very happy about what was coming next for us.

We decided to come off contraception, and I got pregnant after a year. I was starting to think it wouldn't happen for us but it did. We were shocked and felt scared, but we were equally very happy about it. I carried on as normal; riding, shoeing horses, and generally, being very busy. I'd bought Lenny just months before so I continued with his training. He's an impeccably behaved young horse, and we get on so well.

The months were flying by and I was starting to grow a little bump. You didn't like me being so busy, and you really didn't like me riding but I did it all anyway, I was four months pregnant when I fell off Lenny. It was the first time he had ever put a foot wrong, and he bucked until I was chucked out of the saddle and landed harshly on the ménage floor. I was winded and I felt fear almost instantly. *My baby. What have I done?*

After sorting Lenny out, I called you and I told you what had happened. You were so angry, and said those words everyone hates to hear. 'I told you so.' I rested up in the hope that my baby had been protected inside of that fluid-filled sac, but it wasn't to be. Five days before the fall I'd had an amniocentesis, which includes piercing the sac with a very fine needle to withdraw the fluid that surrounds the baby to do tests. We hadn't been sure about it but we were told our baby had a very high risk of down syndrome, and the doctor explained to us that our baby could have moderate-to-severe physical and mental disabilities. We felt scared, and didn't know what to do. We were told it was a very low-risk procedure, and the doctor recommended it, so we went ahead.

Everything went well and with much relief, our baby was perfectly healthy. I was told to take a couple of easy days, which was exactly what I did. After five days of rest, I cracked on as I usually did, and the worst thing that could have happened, happened. The sac had ruptured and I was losing the fluid very slowly.

I was on bed rest for weeks; in and out of hospital. I had reached twenty-one weeks, and I was chuffed. We were starting to get towards a safer gestation, and it filled me with hope. We had brought all sorts of baby things, ready to start his room and get ready for a premature baby. I had been off work ever since and had hardly left the house. I was doing exactly as I was told. My friends were on horse duty, and Michael was running around looking after us, the dogs, and the house while working too.

One night I was sat on the sofa relaxing and my waters broke. I knew from that moment that our boy would die. I felt instant sadness, guilt, and regret. We were in hospital for a week, and I contracted an infection. Our boy had to be induced, which would bring him to his death. It was an emotional delivery and it took over 40 hours. My boy was finally out, and he had died during the labour.

Michael held him in his arms, and he became more and more broken the longer he looked at him. I think I passed out for a while and when I woke up, Michael looked at me with tears streaming down his face. 'He's cold. His body is going cold. Gem, hold him.'

I took him, and I felt sick with grief. My dear son. This perfect little body fully formed in all the right ways. His lungs had failed him. They'd needed to be stronger. My heart broke fully for the first time in my life, and the guilt will never leave me.

Chapter Five

*T*oday I've given up. I'm fed up of feeling this way; sad, and emotional as though I might just burst and never stop crying, and my physical being is aching like it does every day, but today it's too much. It's making me heave and sick. I'm in bed with the dogs, writing in this journal.

Everything around me is you; either what you bought me, handed down to me, or you were with me when I got it. I feel so ill. It's you who would make me better. I'm ill because my aching heart can't cope today. I can't pretend today. I give up, and I hope tomorrow I am stronger.

I can't look at your picture, but I see you in my head. You're laughing and nudging me as you talk. I am sure I am dying inside. I feel like my body is shutting down. I'm in too much pain to function. I wish you had died a different way. How could you have died by your own hands? Removing yourself by choice from us, without a warning. No chance to say goodbye.

I hope I can forgive you one day.

I've been riding most days, and taking Lenny out on long hacks. It's my safe place. I can cry, and I know I won't see anyone. Lenny happily wanders along with me hunched up on his back, crying and chattering to him about nonsense. I get a chance to think a lot while I'm out here. It's peaceful in this countryside. My thoughts wonder from you to Hayley and John. I worry for them because I know they must feel as bad as I do, and I know there isn't anything anyone can do to take it all away.

My future seems so dull. I know I have Michael but I worry for him. What if I'm becoming someone different? What if I turn into someone so different that he no longer loves me?

How could I lose him?

I just want to fall asleep and wake up when it's all over; when I've learnt to be stronger.

We are still waiting for the inquest. I'm dreading it. It will be horrendous to know how much damage you caused your body.

I just cannot believe you killed yourself.

I'm still angry with you; so angry!

I dreamt of you last night for the first time since you've been gone. You were just as I remember; beautiful, vibrant, in the moment, and so happy. Your hair was straightened, with hair spray on your textured layers, and your fringe flicked away to one side, blonde with copper mixed up in there. You had makeup on. You always preferred the natural look. You never wore much but just enough to enhance your facial features. You were wearing casual jeans, boots with a small square heel, and a pastel coloured T-shirt that was nicely fitted.

It was so nice to be with you, hearing your voice, and watching you move like you did. We were speaking but I couldn't hear what you were saying. I don't know why that is? I did feel sad to wake up to the shock of you not being here. But the dream was worth it. It was so good to see you.

Hayley and I saw Kevin today. We seem to dread it but when we are in the room with him, we don't want to leave. He makes us feel safe and normal; most of the time we don't feel normal. Once a fortnight doesn't seem enough but that is all we can afford. The charities are slow, and there is no help out there, which is responsive. We've been waiting for a counsellor for over three months and we are still on the waiting list.

I'm in such a dark place right now. I'm sat here on my living room sofa. I need help. I need to talk to someone. I search up 'suicide survivors' on Google. A helpline phone number comes up on the page. I'm calling them. I'm desperate. I dial the number and I speak to a lady. She seems uneducated regarding the after-effects of suicide. I don't think she has any experience about what I'm going through. It's pointless. I feel like a fool. I won't do that again.

I've been thinking for some time about trying antidepressants but I'm not sure if they will help me.

You were on over twenty tablets a day plus your morphine patch. You had many operations on your back, which altered your life forever. You used to get those leg spasms that would make you shout out with pain and a part of your brain was starting to shut down. The reason was the fifteen-to-twenty years on strong medication and the chronic pain from which you suffered every day.

You never complained of pain, and you always got on as best you could.

The insomnia used to bother you too. You used to iron at 3 am most mornings.

The thyroid problems weren't nice for you either. You especially hated the way it made you feel, and how it made you put weight on, and make your neck swell and that hysterectomy you had five weeks before you died.

I think everything was getting too much for you; the pain, the memory loss, and then your hormones.

You were such a strong woman. You coped without a complaint until the dreaded night it got to be too much.

I remember when I was about fifteen – this was after your major back operation – you were starting to feel a little better, and I was off school for a few days to help look after you, and I took you out for a walk in your wheelchair. You told me that you won't ever end up in a wheelchair, I always wondered to what extent you meant that comment. I think I know now.

You hated the thought of relying on anyone, and I know how much your memory loss was bothering you.

You would go somewhere and forget why, and then laugh about it. You said in your Nottingham accent, 'Oh you'd never guess what I've done now. I went to Bingham and I didn't know why I went. I'm daft aren't I.' You would laugh and roll your eyes. I did think to myself then that you seemed angry at your forgetfulness.

I miss the limp you had, your own way of walking, and I loved it when you would link arms with me. I'd always have to go on the right side of you because you were completely deaf in your left ear. You were partially deaf in your right ear but you managed with your hearing aid.

I remember a time when we were at the local pub and I forgot something so we headed back to your house arm in arm. It was icy and cold. We chatted and laughed. As we walked, we chatted about things that were happening that night, and I slipped over and almost dragged you down with me. I landed right next to a little dog that growled at me as I struggled to get up at speed on the icy ground. You had a laughing fit, and we laughed about that for hours afterwards.

You lost Grandma when she was only fifty-three. I know how this broke your heart. You had to learn about loss at such a delicate age, just seventeen. Your siblings had all left home and grown up. I have only ever heard such wonderful things about Grandma. She was pure with a big heart, kind, and caring. She sounds a lot like you. She had a lovely heart-shaped face, and dark hair with soft facial features. She was from Irish descendants and very Catholic. You were unplanned, weren't you? Grandma was in her late thirties when she had you.

Grandad Ron – I remember the morning you got the phone call, informing you of the news of his passing. Another ache to add to your heart. He was from a poor family, and he fought in the war. He was quite a good-looking man in his younger days. He was well-known for his mischief. He loved his ale, and he smoked a lot. You were all so close. Your brother and two sisters would go away on holidays abroad when you were all well into your thirties and forties. He was such a genuine character, and he was so important to everyone. I love hearing the stories. In one, you were all on the airplane going to Tenerife or Benidorm, the flight pressure was building, and his false eye fell out, rolling around on the floor. Auntie Vivienne had to get on her hands and knees to find it, while everyone was laughing, of course.

I wonder why some people suffer so much more than others?

I wonder if, in time, I'll feel how you felt when you had Hayley and me: Grandma never got to meet us. When I finally have my children, they will never get to meet you, be spoilt by you, and feel your warm and protective nature. I'll have to give them enough love so they can feel you through me. I can do that. You showed me how to. I remember the way you held Jack the night he was born; the love in your eyes and in your body. You were so gentle. I could see how much you loved him.

I found a card you wrote to him.

My little baby Jack,

When I held, kissed, and cuddled you last week I didn't want to leave you, but I know your great-grandma Gladys and great-grandad Ron will hold you tight and look after you until I come to join you.

Sleep tight, my baby angel.

Love your nana and John

xxxxxxxx

After all the non-stop crying, there has been a period of coldness, sharpness, and anger. I've been struggling to cry, and I feel it building up inside of me like a pressure cooker. I can feel it reaching the surface. I think of you. I feel my harsh eyebrows soften and my lips loosening. I think about how much I miss you and the tears start to fall. As I cry, the pain feels unbearable. I'm heaving but nothing is coming up. I can't imagine being without you for any longer. I need you now. When I was younger, I used to worry about how awful it would be to lose you. I couldn't bear the thought of it. I knew one day I would lose you, but, Mum, not like this.

Agony is a fair word to use. This agony is intense. It's all over my body and in my heart.

I'm still off work. I can't imagine going back yet. Shoeing the horses isn't the problem, it is being with the people. Most of my clients, I have shod their horses for around eight to nine years, and I know most of them really well. With this lingering over me, though, it's become awkward and I feel them worrying about upsetting me or saying the wrong thing. I usually love my job, the horses, and the people. I have a lovely old red transporter van that I drive to my clients' yards, farms, or homes. They have their horses ready and are waiting for me with a cup of tea and a chat. We usually chat about what's been happening in-between the shoeing cycle. That's the thing. I see my clients between every four to eight weeks so I know them well. I've got a friend who has covered my shoeing round for me until I'm ready to come back.

I saw your sisters yesterday, Vivienne and Brenda. Trevor, your brother, couldn't make it. They remind me of you in their ways. They are much older than you. They insisted on coming over to the village. Vivienne took two buses to get here and Brenda only lives twenty minutes away but she also had to get a bus. They are both stubborn, so when they say they are coming to us, we don't even argue. Once their minds are made up, that's it. Much like you, Mum. They are distraught to have lost their little sister. You were their baby. Trev is so sad. He is missing you. We know you couldn't help it, but we wish you'd told us how bad you were feeling. Brenda, Vivienne, Hayley and I spoke about you all afternoon. We were all in and out of tears.

Viv says you're in a different dimension. She says you are with us, and you would have been sat with us laughing about the stories we were sharing.

They knew you all of your life. I wish I had that. I wish I'd known you longer. You were so special to so many. You were so special to me.

Viv says each life has a set plan and this is the way it is supposed to go. She says you're with our family now. Are you, Mum?

You and your sisters look so alike, much like Grandma. I imagine how wonderful life would have been if she had lived. Your life would have been so different.

It's strange, the things that come back to you. I remember very clearly our conversation in the kitchen while I was cooking us dinner. I was home for the weekend from Hampshire, where I did my farriery training. We spoke about the suicide of Robin Williams. We'd seen it in the newspaper. I said, in my naivety, 'His poor family. It seems to be such a selfish act. I can't imagine what his family are going through, especially after finding him.'

You responded quickly. 'It's not a selfish act. Imagine how awful Robin felt to be in a position to need to die and leave all of his loved ones behind.'

Did you jump in front of the train because of what I said about Robin's family finding him? So we wouldn't be the ones to find you?

John is sad. I can tell. He's lost without you. He loved you. He's in tears every day. I hope he's not worse because Michael and I have moved out. We stayed for almost three months, and we've been settled back at home in the caravan for a couple of weeks now.

I found your house a comfort but it eventually started to make me feel despair. Your ashes are on the cupboard. I can't bear to look at them. Your picture is in front of them. Your beauty gleams from the photo. That smile melts my heart. You were happy then, I remember. Your smile could light up a room. Even your eyes would be smiling. The photo next to your ashes is one of you and John. I just love it. You're both so happy; you're both laughing in it. I wonder what you were laughing at?

I can see a mark on the glass of that photo. It's from John. He must have kissed it. He has kissed you. How could you leave him like that?

John is a few years older than you. He has dark hair and dark olive skin. You have known him since you were a teenager. He's been friends with Trevor almost all of your life. You both went your separate ways through life and came back together eleven years before you died. You both enjoyed a good night out in the city. I'll miss those nights out. Michael and I would regularly come and meet you for a few drinks and a dance.

When you turned fifty-three, it was a tough age for you. It was the same age Grandma was when she passed away. That's the age you always reckoned you would never live past. You upset me when you told me that but you seemed to mean it. You said it in a way that showed you believed it, and I remember you weren't upset when you said it. When you turned fifty-six, the age you will always stay, I told you we will have you a sixtieth birthday party. You responded in a typical way.

'I won't go. I'm not celebrating being sixty. It's depressing.'

You never did want to get old. Why have you always had such an issue with age?

I'm sitting here at my desk in the caravan, writing to you. I'm listening to Radio2. I can't believe it. On come the Bay City Rollers. Was that you, Mum?

It's made me smile. I can imagine you as a teenager, singing, and dancing away to them, with your homemade black trousers with red-and-white stripes down the side.

Chapter Six

I can't sleep. It's awful. I keep seeing you on the trainline. I watch you drive away from the house. I see you park up and walk up to the tracks. You stand there peacefully, and you wait. The lights are bright as the train approaches you and the horn is blowing over and over. You don't seem panicked. I envision the train hit in to you and throw your lifeless body across the tracks. Those same tracks we used to cross on summery days when Hayley and I were kids. I'm reliving the phone call from John. I think I'm punishing myself because I didn't help you. I feel that same knife puncturing my heart and twisting all over again. My breathing is becoming laboured. I feel like I'm slowly bleeding to death. It would hurt less to be hit by a train.

I texted you today. I don't know why. They will never reach you.

Dear Mum,

I will love you forever and always.

Xxxxxxxxxxxxxxxxxxxxxxxxxxxxx

I wish you could get this.

Xxxxxxxxxxxxxxxx

Michael has organised a reiki session for me. It's today. I feel nervous, and a part of me doesn't want to go. I find myself driving there anyway. It's at her house. I knock on the door and she answers. She seems friendly. I instantly feel better, and now I'm intrigued. I am told to relax and lie down on what looks like a massage table. She is holding her hands above me. I close my eyes and wonder what will happen. It's starting to go dark. My eyes just see dark now, like I'm in a pitch-black room. I feel these bubbles rising up through my body, a bit like when you open a can of coke and all the fizz rises to the top, but this is really slow as the bubbles go through my body up and out. What is it?

Once the bubbles stop, I see you. I'm having a vision of you as a young girl about eight or nine with your mam, Trev, Bren, and Viv. You are all laughing and playing around. You seem cheeky. It's a bit like watching a black and white movie.

The session is over. I feel emotional and I think she can tell. I haven't told her why I'm here and I don't think I want to either. I hand over the money to her, and I thank her. I really mean it. I'm so glad I got to see you like that. She's pleasant, and shows me out. I'm in the van now, Mum, and I'm sad. I cry all the way home.

Nanna has asked me to go with her to the hospital. I'm happy to. It's really nice spending the afternoon just me and her. We never get time like this. We walk into the nurse's room. The nurse asks Nanna a few questions about her leg injury, and then she asks her if she is allergic to anything. Nanna says, 'Penicillin'. The word hit in to me sharp. I wasn't expecting that. You were allergic to that. Whenever we had to get an ambulance for you after a fall, I was always asked if you were allergic to anything, to which I would say, 'Penicillin'.

As the words came from her mouth, I felt an unexpected urge to cry out, fold over, and let out my tears. I felt shocked. This morning had started well. I was feeling positive today but it's shifted harshly into a bad day like all the others.

We are going on holiday to Turkey; Hayley, Paul, and the kids, along with our cousins, Nanna and Grandad. They are family from Dad's side. It's been planned for some time, and I think it's going to be a positive trip. It's what we need.

I found a book in the shop at the airport. It's about a man who lost his wife to terrorism. It looks a tough read but I'm drawn to it. I see her happy, smiling face on the front cover. She is holding a baby in her arms. I bought it, and I've started it. I was right. It is a tough read. I've got to a part in his book where I've stopped to think. He says, 'The only thing that matters is that she is gone. The rest is just background noise.'

I start to think about this and compare it to my grief. To me, the background noise matters. To me, it has made a difference that you killed yourself. You weren't killed by someone else. You didn't have an accident, and you didn't die of a disease. You died because you wanted to. He does go on to say, 'The real tragedy is now taking place: absence.' I feel that; the absence. That's what I struggle most with; the fact that I can't get to you. I can't touch you, see you, or feel you. You're absent and I can't change it.

John seems broken. He doesn't look right anymore. He has lost weight. His face looks sunken and gaunt. The life that you could see in him has gone. I've asked him if he would like to move in with me and Michael when we buy our house. He doesn't want to but I feel better knowing he has the option because I can't bear the thought of him left alone. You left him alone. This is when my anger towards you reaches the surface. It's when I see John and Hayley in utter misery.

Hayley has lost a lot of weight. Her gaunt and skinny face is pale and expressionless. A lot of the time, I catch her staring into nothingness with watery eyes. The life that surrounded her has left her too. She wants to die. She told me so. My anger for you rages. It is like a fire setting alight anything in its path. I'm angry at you, and I want to tell you so, and I can't. I can't because you took the easy way out. We are battling this without you. We are battling this for you, and I hate you for that.

Chapter Seven

*S*ome people I know expect me to be moving on, just four months down the line. They who have not experienced such tragedy want me to move on because I make them feel uncomfortable when I'm with them because they don't know how to act around me. It's just not that simple. Moving on for me isn't in sight at all. You're still always at the forefront of my mind. The anger takes over me regularly and occasionally allows my sadness to creep in. It winds me up and wipes me out.

When people look at me, do they think of me as the one whose mum committed suicide? Do I no longer have my own identity?

I've started to look at my life and think a lot more about what I want to do with it. Maybe I'll start again in a different direction? I've heard that trauma can alter us and because of that, a change must happen if we are to move on. The deeper the experience, the deeper the change. I wonder where I'll end up?

~

Hayley and I have found many feathers, robins, and little things that make us feel like you are with us. Hayley treasures hers. She keeps them in a jar in her kitchen. I usually stamp on mine and cover them with mud or I throw them in the bin. It makes me angry to think of you sending me a message with a feather. You shouldn't be leaving me a feather because you should be here with me.

I can see you. I close my eyes and I can see you. It's morning. I'm still in bed. I'm awake but I feel this strange thing happen to my body. I feel paralysed. I can't move anything but my eyes. I'm awake but I feel as though I'm dreaming. I hear your voice. You say to me in a desperate tone, 'You ok, Gem?' You make me feel safe so I let my mind take me to wherever it is going. I have these visions coming in and out. Your face, and then you're sitting in your favourite chair. Is this real? Can I really see you? Are you trying to take me somewhere and show me something? I see hundreds of different faces. I even see a dog. They are coming towards me and passing me so all the other faces can come too. Some of the faces stop and take me into some kind of story; almost like a film. I open my eyes and I sit up. I look around the room and close my eyes again, and the faces are still coming to me. It's really happening. What does it mean?

I see several different stories. I feel special. I feel lucky that I'm able to see these stories. Are the stories peoples' past lives? Are all of these people dead, like you? I am looking for your face, but I can't find you. I feel scared now, but I wonder if it's you showing me something, and then I have to keep searching.

The faces have ceased and the vision moves on to our local pub. I see the pub. I walk around past the window. I look in, and I see you in there. I see you sitting in a chair next to John and Michael.

Oh my, I'm going to see you. I speed up and I walk into the pub. I rush towards John, Mike, and you. I walk over and I sit next to you. I see you. You're sitting there looking at me. You're wearing a thin-strapped vest top. It's blue and matches your jeans. You look very casual, very relaxed, and happy. I lean over to you and I put my cheek on yours. I feel you. I grab your arm as I collapse into you. 'Mum, I miss you.' Before I get any response, it's over. Everything is gone. It's just me here in this room. I'm awake. I keep closing my eyes but there is nothing. It's all gone.

I've booked in to see the doctor. The appointment is today. I've come to tell her I'm ready to go back to work. I'm sitting here in the waiting area, looking around at the people and wondering what they are here for. Is there anyone here feeling like me? Is there anyone who has experienced what I'm experiencing and survived or is it just me?

Music is playing and I'm hoping it stays cheery because I'm so fragile. I feel frail and weak. It's my turn. My name has buzzed up. I sit opposite her, and she looks at me and says, 'How are you?' She knows from my notes. I look at her as I try to swallow that ball but I can't. It's lifting up and coming out. With that, I burst into tears and I can't stop.

She tells me I'm taking all the right steps towards healing; what with the counselling and dog walking, riding my horses, and having support around me. I don't feel as though I am healing. I think I am just getting used to the pain. She advises me to take some more time off work. I think that is sound advice, and I do have Carl helping me out.

I have seen one of the girls from the stables. She was asking me how I have been coping. I explain simply that I feel the worst is over. The last three months have been tough, and I could not survive that time again. While I'm saying that she looks sad, and says that she can't believe how I've got through it, and she thinks I'm so strong.

I look at her with a pause, a little shocked. I have to be careful. I don't want to upset her. I say slowly and softly, 'I don't have a choice. The only other option is to die. I'm left here to deal with it, and that's all I can do.'

She takes a step back and looks shocked and deeply saddened. She pauses her response. I can see she gets it now, and she nods in agreement.

I woke up again last night at 3.00am. I wake and, in an instant, you're there with your lovely fresh face and hair. You're looking at me as you take the steps towards the train, and there is nothing I can do to stop you. I want to scream at you to stop. I don't know anything about what happened to you. I don't know what you were wearing, if you were crying, or what you did when the train driver was sounding his horn at you in desperation to make you move. I don't know what you looked like when the train impacted your body or where you landed. I'm still awake and it's now 6am.

Michael is up and getting ready for work. I've been reliving everything. The things I should have said to you. Why didn't I call round that night? What were you thinking?

It's October 27th, the second anniversary since Jack died. The loss of you both is too much. I feel broken and exhausted today; but I must go on.

We have been to see Kevin today. He's helping me find the answers to the questions I have for you. My theory is in my head. It's all there but I'm just struggling to find it. What with all the clues that I missed when you were alive; the little clues you would drop into our conversations that I failed to process and link to the depression and then suicide.

I still struggle to understand though. You were so immaculate; perfect for all to see. You hid it from everyone but subtly dropped in the clues of your truth; then you just upped and left, just like that. Gone. Was it different for you, the subtle clues you left us with? Did you think they were screaming out, 'Help!' and no one was hearing you?

I saw John last night. He was so upset. I was brave and I pretended I was fine so I could be the strong one. When I appear strong, I block out the pain, and for that, I am punished. The explosive flood is bursting. I can't hold it any longer. Today is awful. I could die today. I want to die today.

The hate I feel for you is the strongest emotion I have ever felt. What does that make me? Shouldn't I feel only sadness and guilt? I'm going for a walk to try and clear my head. I walk down to the river with my boys, Ralph and Toby. I'm drawn to this tree. I stop under it and I sit. I can't see through my tears. They well up in my eyes and stream down my cheeks. I wish I had the strength to hang myself on this tree. I cry aloud to you, 'I don't forgive you! How can I ever forgive you? I hate you! I hate you! You've passed all this down on to us and we have to deal with it. All your mess is now ours, and we have to carry on and have to live with this without you.' What is the point of life anyway? I wish you hadn't bothered. I wish I had never been given a life. I don't want it.

We sit awhile and I collect myself. Ralph is sat on my knee, and Toby is off chasing rabbits. I think Ralph feels the pain too. He seems to understand. I kiss his head, and he licks my cheek. We must move on before the feeling of death returns to me because I know the strength of the tree and the dog leads would be enough.

We arrive home, and I brew a cup of tea. I feel forced to look at the photos of us. My hate for you eases but my sorrow increases. You're my beautiful mum. We've had such good times. Why wasn't it all enough? Why weren't we enough? I really don't know how long I can stay alive without you.

Chapter Eight

I hurt my finger yesterday. I was leading both the horses and Lenny got trapped by the gate. I wasn't concentrating and he pulled backwards, trapping my ring finger by the knot at the end of the lead rope. It's all swollen up, bruised, and sore. I need to show you so you can tell me what to do with it. I remember when I broke my toe and you strapped it up for me. You gave me that care that only you could give; so attentive and sympathetic, caring and kind. That's why you made such a good auxiliary nurse back when you were younger, before the back problems started. Your love was so strong and deep, and I miss it.

My heart beats fast all the time, and the skin inside my mouth is peeling away. I have ulcers inside my mouth too. I feel weak and shaken, and a panic attack doesn't feel far away. I can't allow myself too much pressure for anything as I may break down and I'm scared. What happens after that?

I had plans to go to my friend's house. A few of us were invited. I found myself sitting on the side of the bed, rocking and shaking. I was sweating and I felt scared to leave Michael. I felt that pressure build like the panic attacks were coming back. It will ease eventually, won't it?

~

I had a dream that I lost Michael. He had died. I woke up in a panic, and he was there asleep next to me, I felt as though I had been given a second chance. I need to learn to appreciate everyone I have left. Is it you, Mum? Are you trying to teach me to move on? I feel as though you are with me. I feel courage and strength, and the hatred is easing.

~

November

I'm back at work now. It's the right time for me, I think.

I have picked three pictures of the two of us to put into your ashes box before we bury you. I stare into your eyes. I can't take my eyes off you. I feel my heart beat faster. My eyes fill and the tears fall. Your face makes me smile, yet my heart can't cope.

We buried you today. I put the rest of Jack's ashes in with yours. The ashes of Jack's that I couldn't bear to lose. We spread him down in Dorset but we kept some of him here with us. Now, he is with you. You're both together in that box under the dirt. There are a few of us here to say our final goodbyes. Each of us adds some pictures of our happy times together. John brought a bottle of prosecco to pour over you once we buried you. I bet you enjoyed that.

You're together now, with your mam, dad, Darren, Brian and Baby Jack. Darren was your nephew, Auntie Brenda's son. He died on that bloody moped, so young; eighteen, wasn't he? And Brian, Daren's dad, Brenda's husband. He died years later, falling down the stairs, and tripping over the dog. I've always wondered how Brenda found the strength to carry on. She's suffered great loss over her lifetime, and especially now, after what you have done to her.

Mum, it was so hard to say goodbye to you again.

I wrote you a letter and buried it with you.

Mum,

We are here to finally put you at peace.

We thank you for the messages, the signs, and the feathers that you have sent us.

We will treasure our memories with you always until we see you again.

We ask you now, please, be at peace and now rest with our family that have already left us, but we ask you two things. We ask you to come back every now and then to pay us a visit and leave us a sign, and we ask you to send our love to the others.

You are so loved, my dear mum, forever and always xxxxxx

Do you remember when I told you about the saying I heard when I was around twenty? 'Youth is wasted on the young.'

You said, 'Yes, that's so true.'

I thought I understood what it meant, but I didn't. It's only now I truly understand it. I feel it. If I knew what I know now, I think I would have changed a few things.

This life is relentless. I'm empty, and I have no purpose. I'm starting to like the thought of taking drugs; the kind that make you forget it all. At least I could have a break from this dull, empty existence that I feel every moment of the day. Life is no longer a gift. It is hard work. Life is wasted on me now. I wish I could give it to someone who could make use of it. I hate that I'm lucky enough to breathe, see, and feel, and I don't want any of it. The only reason I'm still alive is because what my death would do to our family and my animals. If I didn't have them, I would have followed you, Mum, and I'd be out of this agony. I have never felt so lifeless. There's feeling of constant heaviness through my body; every step I take is slow, and I feel like I'm dragging myself around with a fake smile. The pale face and black bags under my eyes tell the story of pain and sleepless nights. It's been four months now and all I want is to move on and bury it, but I don't know how to. Maybe I am on borrowed time. Does my mind have a limit on this uncontrollable pain that is so constant it never subsides? Mum, is that how it was for you?

I want a terminal illness, and I wish it would hurry up and take me away. Happiness is so far away from me now. I can't see it anymore.

This song makes me think of you:

By Mumford and sons, *Reminder*.

Don't let me darken your door

It's not what I came here for

And I won't hear you cry when I'm gone

I won't know if I'm doing you wrong

A constant reminder of where I can find her

A light that might give up the way

Is all that I'm asking for without her I'm lost oh my love don't fade away

So watch the world tear us apart

A stoic mind and a bleeding heart

You never see my bleeding heart

And your lights always shining on

And I've been travelling oh so long

Mum, these words were made for you.

My sorrow is so deep today. It's so deep it's all I can feel. The sadness is excruciating and I'm dying inside.

I gave in to myself and I'm now on antidepressants. I need something to take the edge off and ease the sharpness of these feelings. The doctor said the first two weeks will be the hardest, but I can't possibly feel any worse than this so, I'm not worried. I've quickly gone from the sharpest of pain into nothingness. I feel empty and numb. I told Kevin about my feelings of nothingness. All my mixed-up emotions are still and quiet. I don't feel pleasure nor do I feel pain. I just feel empty. I also told him about Jack. I feel I can trust him now.

Michael's mum made me a cushion out of your wool. It's so beautiful. It reminds me of you; the colours and the way it feels. She came over for a few hours. She has gone home now. Michael is outside so I look at the cushion. It makes me smile, and I glance at the picture book Hayley's made for me. It's all pictures of you. I smile at your picture. I open the book. I'm feeling strong enough. I look at the first picture; it's you, me, Hayley, and Olivia. Your face, your beautiful, smiling face, staring back at me makes the tears stream, and I fall to the floor.

Michael is out for the night. He's called and is ready to be picked up. I drive out and it's dark, really dark. I feel so panicked. I'm scared that someone will jump out in front of me and I'll kill them like the train driver killed you. My heart is pounding, and I can't help but feel so scared. I can picture someone stepping out from the bushes and waiting to be hit by me to meet their end.

I've been on the tablets for over a week now and I feel a lot more 'with it'. I feel my emotions are more controlled. I can't cry anymore though. Is that bad? I feel sad, and I feel I need to cry but I can't. I'm angry but I'm not angry at you anymore, Mum. You were the beating heart of the family. You made Christmas, and you made birthdays. Whenever we moved house or were ill or accomplished anything, you were always there. We never had to ask. You would just be there ready to support, celebrate, or boss us around and tell us how it should be done.

I remember when you went away on holiday. You invited me over the night before to show me what to feed the cat and dogs and to basically show me how to run your house because you insisted I moved in. You wouldn't let me have your dogs at my house. I had to bring my dogs to yours and move in. You got carried away showing me around the house I already knew so well; showing me how the heating works, and the hot water, and you even showed me how to turn on the lights. At that point, I burst out laughing, and you said, 'Yeah, ok. You get the point'.

You used to make me and Hayley do chores. One time, when I was a kid around eleven years old, I was ironing a shirt and you came over to show me how to do it. I sat back and watched you iron all of it while you were telling me how to do it. You loved things to be done properly, I was a little half-hearted back then, and only did as little as I needed to.

We saw Kevin today. He told us to bring in three photos each, ones which are important to us. One of my photos was the one of me, you, Hayley, and Olivia at my wedding party. I told him about my guilt; the guilt that I see every time I look at that photo. I had Jack growing inside of me in that picture. The guilt has eaten away at me. The fact that I killed Jack, and the fact that I was so consumed by my pain I didn't notice yours, and I wasn't there for you. If I had listened to you in the first place, and didn't ride the horses, and Jack had survived, I wonder if you would still be here?

We told him about your kindness, and what we have learnt from you. The three pictures we each brought in were the same ones. We didn't realise until we got them out; three strong memories we both have of us and you.

He said I'm not as detached as he'd once thought. I guess that's a good thing. Kevin said I must go with the emotion when it hits me. I've been pushing it away. But, Mum, it hurts so much. When it comes, it overpowers me and breaks me, and the pain is unbearable. He tells me to remember that it will pass. 'Just think, when it's engulfed you, it will pass.'

Mum, you would be so mad. I've lost my purse. You used to say how I always lost everything, and you never understood how I did. Why do I? Maybe I don't care enough about things, or is it that I just forget? You weren't like that. You never lost anything.

Hayley told me that she doesn't think she could kill herself even though she wants to. If she does, I'll never be able to forgive you. You would have been the one to put the idea in her head. I'd never forgive you if she lost her life to suicide too.

There is a song that makes me cry every time I hear it. It fills me with that guilt. 'Say something, I'm giving up on you.' The guilt that is in me because you didn't ask for help but I failed to recognise that you needed it. Were you too tired to ask for help? Were you just too tired to live any longer?

My goodness, the hole I have inside of me is truly a broken heart. The love I have for you has nowhere to go. I can't give it to you anymore, and you can't give me yours.

I am so lost.

Wherever you lived, I followed you. You were always just down the road from me. And now, you're nowhere to be seen. We moved around a fair bit when we were younger; here, there, and everywhere. We would live in these places for a few years, sell up and move on. You made money on each house you bought and slowly worked your way up the housing ladder. Finally, when I moved home from Hampshire, I wanted to stay close to you, so Michael and I rented a house just down from where you lived.

The meditating is teaching me that the sky is always blue and sometimes clouds come along and cover the blue sky; it's usually thin foggy clouds but sometimes there are jet-black and angry clouds but eventually, the clouds thin and ease and the blue sky is always there. I hope I can find my blue sky one day, but I hope more that Hayley can find hers.

I read somewhere, 'In great loss, there is always love, and the gift of kindness is found deep within after such an experience is suffered.'

I guess if there is kindness somewhere within and a terrible experience is suffered, that must give you greater empathy, and then that is when the kindness is found.

Will I find my gift of kindness or will this experience make me bitter and angry?

You found your gift of kindness. Did you find that when you lost Grandma?

I'm trying so hard to figure it all out, work through each process as it hits me, but it hurts way too much. It's easier for me to block it out, block you out. Kevin said it's not healthy and if I block you out now, I'll never be able to think of you because when I do there will only be pain. If I work through the pain now, go with it and feel it, I'll be able to think of you and smile.

During November, I've mostly been empty and numb. I think of you every minute of every day but I don't feel much inside. My brain isn't allowing me to think about you much other than the outline of you. I don't know what December will bring. I can only imagine this numbness will turn into a month's worth of emotional outbursts, and as Christmas is approaching, I know it's going to be such a tough one but we have to pretend for Olivia and Harry. Hayley told me the other day that Olivia had a melt down again because she wants you and she's knows you won't be there at her birthday or Christmas. You were always there for her and Harry, and now they have to somehow get used to you not being around ever again.

I told someone how you died, and she said to me, 'How are you at work and functioning? You're so strong'. But it's not that I'm any stronger than anyone else. I'm just so aware that if I stop and give up, it will be so much harder to get back up again, and I'm so scared if I go that way, what I may do when I'm down there, I have the potential to die by choice and I cannot let that happen.

~

Hayley rode Deano today. I know how much you loved him. I'm hoping Hayley can put some of her energy and affection into him, I think it will help her. Deano and Lenny help me. I've got your riding boots and hat. Sometimes I like to wear them. I feel in some way that I'm wearing them for you, like I'm taking you out for a ride.

I got a tattoo for you. I know how much it would have angered you. You didn't like tattoos, but I hope it's annoyed you a little because that was our thing, wasn't it, Mum? You always told me not to do things and I always did them anyway. I always liked to learn from my own mistakes, just like you; stubborn in our own quiet ways.

I got the words off that song as a tribute to you.

'So watch the world tear us apart, a stoic mind and a bleeding heart.'

It's to the left of my rib cage. It hurt in a stingy kind of way.

And I got these words to symbolise the love I have for Michael: 'Love; it will not betray you, dismay or enslave you. It will set you free.'

You would have loved those words. I remember you used to search for ages to find a card that had the right words in it so you could get your point across to the person the card was for, to show them how much they meant to you. You have always been like that, haven't you? So kind and so tough. You've taught me to be so strong in my mind. If I choose not to show someone my emotions, I can block them from the outside world, no one would ever know I was in such turmoil. But you have now taught me that it is so important to at least show someone or a small selection of people, so you can share the pain, and in some way ease it.

I used to look after you when you had your many operations. I do remember the first time I was off school, looking after you. I was about ten years old. I was sitting downstairs watching nickelodeon while you were resting upstairs in bed. I heard a loud bang and I had to argue with myself to get up and go upstairs to check on you but I was glad I did. You had fallen over going to the toilet and you couldn't move. I called for an ambulance but I was crying so hard I couldn't speak and you had to take the phone off me even though you could hardly breathe. I was a mess, I thought you were going to die. And the handful of times I called ambulances for you, and was in A&E all day with you because you had fallen down the stairs and the metal in your back could have been shifted and could paralyse you. You had to wear that awful neck brace and be lying on the hard stretcher, not able to move or go the toilet until you had the X-ray to show the metal was still in place. The handful of times you fell over and broke those poor arthritic fingers of yours. And the number of times you would stub your poor toes; the massive bunions you had because of all the years wearing inappropriate shoes that you wore in the name of fashion.

Hayley and I have got your shoes now. They have been worn into the shape of you. The way you wore your right shoe differently to your left. That leg was shorter because of the amount of bone you had removed from your hip to go into your spine, and how the bunion shape has been embedded into both shoes. I love to assess the worn pattern of them, and it reminds me so intimately as to how you would walk and move. Hayley, Olivia, Harry and I are from you and we will make you so proud every day. We all have little traits from you. Yesterday, Olivia was doing your voices. She did them so well, and she clearly put so much thought into them. Harry is interested in space now, and I think it's because he thinks you are a star along with Baby Jack and his grandad Michael. I've bought him a telescope for Christmas so he can look at you all.

Ralph's hair has grown back now. You will be pleased about that. It would have upset you to imagine your baby Ralph in such distress. You and Ralph were very alike, always getting injured, and never complaining about it. He loved you so much, and he misses you. Since you've been gone, when we go to your house, he doesn't ask for treats anymore like he used to. I remember when he asked you and you always gave him at least two, and I'd always have to tell you to not give him anymore but I know you would sneak him another one.

Mum, I'm pregnant! I wish you were here for me to tell you and see the delight in your face. I have just found out, so I'm about two to three weeks. I told Hayley first even before Michael. It's because I wasn't 100% sure and wanted to do another test before I told him. This pregnancy is going to be a tough one. I know any pregnancy I have will be hard after Jack and the miscarriage, but I know you won't be here to help me through and help me when the baby comes. We are all so overjoyed to find out about this new life. I think it will help us all. Another little piece of you, joining the world, can only be such a wonderful gift. I feel blessed and so lucky to be pregnant; my body is developing this little life, and I feel excitement along with fear. I hope this baby makes it.

I have come off the antidepressant tablets because they are not good for the baby. I've only been on them for six weeks but I'm so scared to come off them. How will I cope?

I've been waking up every night around three and I struggle to fall back to sleep. It makes me so tired the next day. As soon as I wake, I feel that terrible shock hit me again, but I still feel detached almost like it's not me who feels the shock. I can't really explain it but when I think about you, I feel as though I'm thinking about a close friend who lost their mum. It brings me a lot of pain but nowhere near as much when I cry. It almost allows me to realise the truth; that it was you who died in that way. Is there something wrong with me for feeling this way?

When I talk to John or Hayley about you, they well up and shed a tear but I feel as though I'm like a stone, dry, hard, and emotionless. I just talk about you like I knew you through a friend or something. Occasionally, it hits me fully, and I feel as though I'm drowning again and it's unbearable. Has my mind decided to protect me from such discomfort, and so I detach myself from the situation?

When people ask how you died, I've started telling them, because when I tell them, I feel no emotion so, I don't have that fear anymore of breaking down in front of them.

Hayley says she doesn't know how I do it, but it's not a choice for me to act this way. I am scared though. What if this is making the healing process so much longer and harder? I worry I've developed some kind of wall that, once it's fully built, I'll never be able to knock it down and feel all the good and bad things that come with emotion.

I'm so tired yet my eyes are wide awake. It's 3.09am now and I'm sick of this, and I'm sick of the constant pretence that all is ok because it isn't.

Christmas isn't far away and everyone around me is getting excited about it. I know Hayley and John aren't, and I'm not feeling anything about Christmas. All I know is we have to pretend for the children. I'll be so happy and excited for them just like I am every time I see them. They are so precious to me. I love them just like I'd love my own.

Maybe I'll try and cry tomorrow. That will release some of this dead emotion that I feel. I know it will bring such a strong outburst of anguish but that must make me feel a little relief after? I'll have to set triggers for myself. I will play the song I chose for your funeral and look at your picture. That will be enough. I've been struggling again to look at your picture because my mind knows that your face is too painful for me to look at and absorb the wonderful memories that each picture brings me.

When I look at myself in the mirror, I see someone very different to who I used to see, I see the bags under my eyes, which I have developed over the five months, and I see new creases around my nose and on my brow from the new position my face finds itself sitting a lot of the time. It's all very subconscious and natural. How grief is so physical.

I remember before Jack died, I used to take lots of photos. I always wanted to capture every moment of my life and the people in it. I don't take photos anymore. Is it because the moment that I used to love to capture has passed? Maybe I don't want to capture the pain and pretence on a picture because I'll be able to see it.

In the coroner's report, it said you told the doctor that your children are keeping you safe but you feel as though they would be better off without you. Three days later they discharged you because you decided you were going to be fine managing alone and they believed you were not a threat to yourself. I'm not happy about that discussion at all. Mum, I wish you'd asked us if we thought we would be better off without you.

I watched a true story about a man who lost his legs in a terrorist attack. I can't help but feel how lucky his family are. Yes, he lost his legs but he's still alive. They feel hope as they go into his room and he's still alive.

I feel sick to my stomach that I have a memory of the night I found out about you. There was no hope of your survival because you were already gone, dead at the scene. It was so quick and so tragic. We had no hope of ever seeing you again.

I dreamt of you again, Mum. You were there, right in front of me, looking as you always did, happy, well-groomed, and smart. I told you I was pregnant. You didn't look shocked as you replied that you already knew. I need you to look after us. Your first act from another dimension. You need to make sure this one makes it. We all need this baby to survive.

To learn how mentally strong you are, you have to be in such a terrible place and you have to work hard, the hardest you've ever had to, and find your way back out of it. I'm working hard to find my way back out of this. I won't be the same but I don't think I want to now. I'm working to become someone better, for you. I know one day I'll be strong enough to help someone else.

Christmas is three days away. I was driving to work and I could feel the tennis ball in my throat growing and my heart was pounding faster. The physical pain is rising and I have to pull the van over. The outburst is so strong, I throw my face into my steering wheel and it all pours out. The knife in my heart is twisting, and the pain is increasing. I've lost you, Mum. I don't feel you around me anymore. I feel so lost without you, and I miss you constantly. This feeling is unbearable. I still wish I could die. I don't care how. I just want to be gone.

Christmas has been and gone. It was extremely difficult to smile and pretend that I'm enjoying myself. I think the kids enjoyed it. They had a moment of sadness while they remembered how you used to spoil them with mountains of gifts; each one of them perfectly wrapped with crisp edges, and each one with ribbons and a tag. Your precise handwriting very neat, and written above a ruler for the perfect straight line.

I remember to myself that I was sitting in the exact same position when you handed me the bag with my leather journal in.

Michael and I have been for the scan today. We get to have an early scan because of the past two babies. It's around seven weeks old, and its little heart is beating good and strong, and everything seems to be healthy. I feel such love for my tiny baby. This new life will bring me a purpose, and maybe they will look a little like you. The baby is due just ten days after your 1st anniversary. It would be a gift to be born on the same day. Do you think it would change the sad feeling somehow?

It's New Year's Eve and I'm feeling very sad. The realisation sinks in that we are at the end of the year 2017. It's the final year I would have been with you. Michael and I stay at home and play a game together. They sing the song at midnight on TV, and I kiss Michael. I cry a little. That song reminds me of you. We usually spent New Year's Eve together and crossed arms and sang the song. If we were apart on New Year's we would ring each other. The lines would always be busy so it would take about ten minutes to actually get through, and you would shout in your high-pitch drunk voice down the phone to me, 'Happy New Year, babe!'

I dreamt about you last night. We were looking through some pictures and you said to me, 'That was spring. You know, before I did it.' I asked you if you regretted it. You said, 'No,' in a very abrupt way. You went on to say it was because you really couldn't see how you could have carried on and coped. I felt relief that you didn't regret it because it couldn't be changed now.

I woke up last night and felt the shock again. I woke and burst into tears. I didn't want to wake Mike up so I went into the living room while I cried. I felt panicked for a while but then I started to see things again. I was scared. I could see shapes, shadows, and colours. I felt lost, panicked and broken. I became hysterical and poor Michael had to witness it. He managed to calm me down. He said it's awful because it reminds him of the early days after you died. We chatted for a while and he put some music on to listen to. I felt the hysteria coming back. I tried to keep it away but it hit me again.

I'm sick of floating around, pretending to get on with the things I always used to before you died. I hate it all now because you're no longer here. I failed to see you were broken, and you took your life away. I hate everything about it. I want to run away from here and never come back to this awful place. I hope the panic attacks haven't harmed the baby. I don't know what I would do if this baby dies.

I wish I could turn it off. Have a break from it, from you; from the way you tore my heart out. Things will get better, eventually, won't they? I think I've got to accept, forgive, and move on. I do hope I can forgive you. Otherwise, I may hate you for the rest of my life.

We saw Kevin today. He gave me some mind tools to help with the panic attacks. He explains that our minds are in two sections; we have the ape side and we have the memory side. Trauma can be stored in the memory side, and the ape side takes it occasionally and presents signs of PTSD.

So, tools to help subside the panic attacks; hold something and think about what it feels like and what it's made of. Control your breathing by counting the breaths and slowing them down. Listen to the noises around you and think about what they sound like, and where they are coming from.

Olivia is sad. She's been asking why you had to die when you weren't old, and she asked if John knew you were dying. She wanted to know if you'd died in bed.

I feel sorry for her. She said she smelt your perfume last night while she was in bed. She explained how she moved the quilt over for you, so you could sleep with her if you wanted to. Olivia is a sweet girl. She's very much like you. She reminds me of you in the things that she does; the way she speaks to the animals, and the way she loves her clothes and dressing up nice.

Olivia is suffering so much. How can we help her? Professionals say it's best to tell them the truth. How can we tell them how you died? Their inexperienced brains having to process that sort of information. The way you left those lovely little people is unforgivable. You meant the world to them and now you're gone. You have broken them like you have everyone else.

Karen, she's your niece, Brenda's daughter. She messaged me to say she and Brenda were upset again about you last night. You are Brenda's baby sister. Your loss has affected so many people in such a negative way. Did you really think we would all get over you or not be that upset? You've ripped our family into pieces, and we've all got to build ourselves back up again. We all feel so terrible that we didn't help you, and that we didn't know how bad you were.

I had another dream of you last night. I was pulling out of a yard at work, and you drove past me in a little old car. It made me wake up instantly. Are you alive? Did you pretend to die? My mind is playing tricks on me. It's something to help my heart and head cope by subconsciously creating hope.

I'm starting to believe you had an illness, something that no one could see, and it took you away from us like a cancer gone unnoticed. We need to learn to live the life that you gave us; the way you would want us to. You were blessed with a full life. It was full of happiness, love, and laughter until the final few months before the illness kicked in. This is how I need to visualise the end of your life. It's the only way I can understand it.

We had our twelve-week scan, Mum. The baby had a strong beating heart and seemed so happy. It was jumping around all over its filled sack of fluid. You would have cried with joy, Mum. I feel a lot better about it now. We are going to be ok. And we will have a happy future together remembering you.

Olivia said she only remembers your face and nothing else. She says she wants to remember all of you, not just your face. Poor little Livy. You would feel so sad to see her this way.

I feel like I am starting to come to terms with it now. I'm left missing you. That's a more normal emotion, isn't it?

I'm sorry I've not written to you for a while. I have been feeling like I don't want to get myself into it because it's too messed up. I have been coping.

We had our third scan. We have been allowed to have several extra scans, and we are with the same consultant as when I was pregnant with Jack. I'm seventeen weeks pregnant now, Mum, and the baby is a little boy. I could have cried when the doctor told me. She's a nice doctor. I told her about you and how you died. She was taken aback because she remembers you. She told me I did well coming off the tablets when I did but, if I need help, I need to tell them. I have support around me though. I think I will be ok. I've suffered so much since you passed and I believe I can get through anything now. I feel positive that I will be ok and will be able to look after Ronnie. That's his name, Mum. We are naming him after Grandad Ron, your dad. You would have loved that. I can imagine you talking to him in that soft voice you had.

I'm still feeling ok, and at the moment I believe that it wasn't anyone's fault, especially yours, that you had to die. I'm trying hard to enjoy life as best I can. I remember you constantly throughout my day, and it usually makes me smile. I am aware that this positive mood will change and the hate for you will come back but I'm enjoying it while I can.

I talk to Dad a lot about you. He helps me so much when I need him. You would be so proud of him for being there. I know that you would have already known that. He's always been there for us, hasn't he?

We are buying our first house, and can finally get out of this caravan. How come everything is happening for us since you've been gone? Are you up there putting things in place for us? Sending us Ronnie and the tiny cottage we fell in love with but someone outbid us. I know you would have said it's not practical for a family home because it's too small and you would have told us not to buy it. One week later, we found the perfect family home down the road from where we are now. You would have liked this one. Is it you? I guess I'll never know until I'm up there with you.

I've not been to your grave since your birthday. That was a hit for us; the fifth of January just after Christmas and New Year. I'm not sure why I don't like going; I've wondered if it's because I can't stand to look at the dirt and think of you under there with Jack. I like to think of you floating in and out of my life, and bringing members of our family with you. Almost like magic, you can see us but we can't see you. You can make us feel you are around sometimes though, and leave us little signs along the way. You're gone from this life but you're not gone from my life, and Ronnie will know everything about you. He will feel like he knew you himself. Olivia and Harry will tell him what life was like when you were in it.

Harry is a darling, Mum. He has got your empathy. He saw a handbag and said, 'Nanna used to wear bags like that and she used to keep treats in there for us'. The kindness that beamed off you like a shining light was infectious and has been passed to all who were around you.

John is doing ok. Some days he looks pained, and other days he looks to have control. He's started moving some things around, and you would be proud of him. They look really nice. He speaks of you a lot, which is really nice because they are all lovely memories that he has, and I remember you telling me the stories so, it's nice to hear them from him too.

Hayley and I have sorted through all of your clothes. That was a tough task. I felt sick throughout. We would smell each item of clothing in the hope we could get one last inhalation of your scent. We found the odd strand of hair too. That would start the tears again.

We have decided to sell your clothes to raise money for a piece of jewellery each with your ashes in it, just like the ring you and Hayley had done for me with Jack's ashes. I remember that. You both raised the money from the generosity of all the family chipping in.

I'm going to get a necklace, a blue stone sat within gold to match Jack's ring. Hayley is getting a ring; a black stone within white gold.

I can picture you saying to us, 'Just get rid of them.' You were brutal like that; extremely sentimental yet you could just throw things out. You had so many clothes and you looked after them so well. Each item was perfectly ironed and hung up, or folded immaculately in ordered rows.

We have kept the special clothes that bring us strong memories, like the dress you wore at Hayley and Paul's wedding, and the dress you wore at my wedding party. There were some others too. I am having them made into a blanket. It's a surprise for Hayley.

We found some of the things you had for Jack. You never showed me these. I suppose when he died you stored them away. They are so beautiful and so special. We will give them to Ronnie. I couldn't love you more if I tried.

When I see trains pass, I wonder if that train was the one that hit you. I watch the speed of them. It makes me shudder. They don't look like they go that fast. I hope you died instantly with no time to feel the pain or any regret.

I'm not sure how much longer I can write to you. It hurts too much. We are in the seventh month; seven months in a world without you. It has been heart-wrenching with strong feelings of it being impossible to get through the next hour and survive without ending it all myself. Please, let me know the worst is over?

Time is passing. I take each day at a time. I see Hayley several times a week, and we speak of the phone many times a day. She is my best friend. Do you remember when it was the three of us? We looked like sisters. She is so much like you. She doesn't look like you, but she acts a lot like you in the things she does.

When the knife that lives in my heart starts twisting again, I hold my bump and I am reminded that I have a little bit of you growing inside me, and I can't wait to meet him, this precious little person.

John had a bad day on Saturday. I could tell. I carefully wrote out a text message and I sent it to him. My aim was to send him courage to get through this bad day.

John, I have been thinking about what you said when you told me you think it was your fault, and I know since, you have said you don't feel it's your fault anymore but, John, you need to know it was never your fault. It was none of our faults, not even Mum's. She never would have wanted to leave any of us. She loved us with her whole heart, and she wouldn't want us to feel any guilt about the past or moving on. We have to find the strength to be happy in a world without her. We need to create a good life that would make her proud. None of us will ever forget her. She was the most precious gift, and we will cherish the time we had with her! We love you, John, I hope you can find happiness again one day.

He told me he misses you, and it's hard when you've had the best. You were his love, his soul, and his life, and he's trying so hard to survive. I can't help but wonder if he wants to die like I do?

Did you know how much he loved you?

I realise now that the life I had with you, can only be spent with the memories I have in the photos and in my head. This realisation is a starting point for me if I am to move on from the darkness. The life I have could be good if I make it happen. I need to banish the memory of how you died and remember the good; to be the person you created, the woman Michael married, the daughter Dad brought up, the sister Hayley grew up with, to be the auntie Olivia and Harry remember and be the mother Ronnie deserves. I have got a responsibility to myself and everyone else to be ok with this life. I am slowly learning that I can be strong enough.

Chapter Nine

It's just so hard because I miss you so much. Yesterday was a tough day. It sounds stupid but I was at the dentist, having a local anaesthetic for my tooth, and a memory hit me. Do you remember I was always so scared of that needle? You would sit in the room with me every time I went to the dentist but, this time, I was there in the chair and I was alone. After this, I was in a downwards spiral for the rest of the day. I walked the dogs and just sat quietly all night. I kept waking up, feeling as though I'm going to get the sleep paralysis again but it didn't come. I was sweating a lot because I was tormenting myself about you; visualising you dead and torn up on my bedroom floor. It's so disturbing.

It's the 3rd of March. Hayley is thirty-one today. She's struggling. She told me she thinks it would be ok if she wasn't here so she could be with you. Mum, I cannot believe you have implanted this option into her head. I tell her I will always be here for her. Hayley is finding life difficult. I'm praying for her. I have never prayed before but I figure where's the harm in trying. I hope it will get better for her.

Mum, we had our twenty-week scan today. Ronnie was so active, and we even got to see him drinking. You would have loved watching him. I wish you were there with us, asking all the right questions, and loving what you saw. He's growing really well and is just right. I hope you can see him and I hope you can show Jack his little brother.

I have hardly slept for five nights. It reminds me of the early days. Last night, I had that sleep paralysis thing happen again. It's terrifying. I have a vision of you on the floor by the bed after you were hit. It torments me, and makes me sick and heave.

I look through the old pictures because I need to box them up ready for the move. They start me crying; your face and your smile. The pose you had is identical to the pose in the pictures of when you were a teenager. It's never changed. Dad came over to tell me the story behind the photos; the ones of when you were young. There are all those memories in the box of photos. Dad has brought the photos alive with the stories.

I found a photo of you and Michael in Benidorm. You were both laughing hard. I remember that night, and the laughs we had on that holiday. You loved Michael like he was your son. He is special, isn't he, Mum?

Ronnie is now the exact same gestation as Jack was when he was born; twenty-one weeks and six days at 6.02pm. You would have had that written on your calendar, and you would have bought me some flowers and a nice vase.

Hayley and I have been talking about the possibilities of emigrating to New Zealand. Hayley told me she remembers when Paul was talking about going for a job interview, which would take them to Australia. She asked you for advice and you told her to go for it. Even though that would have broken your heart, you selflessly wanted them to go for a better life.

It's taken me just over eight months to write on social media. Mental health and suicide are all over the radio, and I feel I must say something.

In memory of all those lost

#mentalhealthawearness

#suicideawearness

When someone you love dies by their own hands, and you find all that is left is loss, anger, rage, sadness, overwhelming guilt, self-blame, and unanswered questions.

Finding post-traumatic stress, depression, and anxiety a new everyday battle.

Unspeakable sadness becomes an ongoing circle of never-ending bewilderment, pain with flashbacks, sleepless nights, and halluci-nations.

Searching for something you've never had to seek before, hope.

Usually, the goal of suicide is not to end life but to end suffering.

People may think that suicide is a choice but a serious mental illness limits the choice.

Dedicated to all those lost to suicide

'Don't let me darken your door,

It's not what I came here for,

And I won't hear you cry when I'm gone, I won't know if I'm doing you wrong.

A constant reminder of where I can find my light that might give up the way,

It's all that I'm asking for without it

I'm lost oh my love, don't fade away,

So watch the world tear us apart,

A stoic mind and a bleeding heart,

You've never seen my bleeding heart.'

If there is ever any doubt speak out. Call a family member a friend or the Samaritans 116 123.

John and Hayley have let me know the report for your inquest has arrived. Hayley and John read it but I can't. I don't want to. This must mean we will be getting the date soon for the inquest. I still haven't decided if I want to go.

Hayley has called me to tell me she has read it, all of it. She is upset. She asks me if I want to know anything. I did. I don't know why but I need to know if your body was in one piece at the end; most importantly, I wanted to know if your head was still attached to your body. It was, thank God. I felt relief but the answer led me to another question. I need to know if all your limbs were still attached. The answer was no. I freeze and feel the blood drain away from my face. It makes me feel spaced out somehow. *Oh no, why did I ask?* I have to leave it there. I can't hear anything else. We are both a mess so we end the call. I can't help but picture the police wandering up and down the train line, looking for your detached body parts. My God, your blood must have been everywhere. Isn't it horrific, Mum? The vision makes me feel sick and pained. My forehead is crinkled up and my heart pounds with too many beats.

The rage starts the rise up my body, and I feel my cheeks turn from pale grey to bright red. I'm angry at you and, again, I hate you for it. I'm sitting in my van and I feel debilitated and stuck. I can't move. I hope no one can see me sitting here, frozen with horror on my face.

The days pass and I slowly absorb the information. It is haunting me. It's unspeakable and it's terribly horrific. I'm finding myself so angry at you. My fists tighten and I'm disgusted by you for what you've done to us. I can't sleep again. I visualise the truth of the night and I see it all. I can see you after. The anger is crippling me. I want to smash your house up; all your lovely things. I want to take a sledgehammer to it all.

May 10, 2018. The inquest is here. I'm not going. I can't sit there and listen to it. I'm still raging at you. Hayley, Paul, John, and Viv have gone. We all met for a drink and have lunch before. I can hardly bear it. We are all fighting our own bodies, our own minds, and we all have this brave exterior. They go in and I'm left to wander around town. I wait and I wait. It's taking hours. I mostly sit outside on the concrete wall, watching lives pass by. So much is happening out here. No one walking past me has a clue why I am sitting here, and I can't help but wonder if anyone else passing me by has suffered in the way I am.

I see them come out, teary-eyed and shocked as the light hits them. I want to ask them what happened but I can't. We go for a drink and they start to talk. They tell me things you said to the doctors, the crisis team, and to them. I no longer feel angry at you. I feel as though you thought about suicide a lot, and how you would do it but you didn't plan it that night. You were intoxicated on alcohol, and along with your recent hysterectomy, and all the daily medication you were living on, you decided at the last minute, 'You know what? I'm not doing this anymore.'

Which is why we didn't get that letter I so wish you'd written, and why your final goodbyes to us weren't full of the love and sadness because you would have known that you were leaving us. You made that last-minute decision when you were out of your mind mentally and added alcohol to that. There was no thought for us at the end, and you did what you thought was right.

Mum, I miss you more than I can express and I'll share everything about you with Ronnie. I'll bring him up how you brought us up. One thing I'll change though is, I won't hide the truth from him. I won't protect him from the truth. I'll tell him one day why you died, and he will know that in our family, we have to be honest and we can get through anything as long as we speak and do it together. No one can harbour such pain and despair and survive.

I'm here, Mum, in hospital. I've been admitted because Ronnie is laying transverse and it's a very dangerous position for him. He's thirty-seven weeks gestation now. He's fully formed and safe to come into the world. The doctors want him to stay in there for as long as possible. They are going to schedule me for a C-section at thirty-nine weeks.

Your anniversary is slowly creeping up on us, and I'm aware Ronnie may be born on the same day. I'm struggling in here mentally. I think of how you died too much and I'm very emotional.

The midwife has just been to see me, and she gave me the date for the C-section, it's the 25/07. As she says the date with a smile, I pretend and smile as I say, 'Thank you'. It's the same day. As I'm going over what it will mean for Ronnie every birthday, I think to myself, 'It's ok. We will make it happy for him.' But I feel that darkness, that cloud, start to creep over me. It's heavy on my chest and I find it hard to breathe.

As the evening draws and I finally fall asleep, I wake up in a panic at 4am. Of course, he can't be born on that day. His birthday can't be that day. I need to tell them. I need them to know now. I walk down the corridor and I find a midwife. I tell her why I can't have that day. The tears stream down my face, and she looks so sad. She hugs me. She assures me it won't be that day. We talk and she makes me some tea. I feel better now.

Michael's mum and sisters visit me most days. They are very precious to me, even though I find it hard to show it. Dad is here most evenings, and Michael is here every day. Some days he just sits next to me while I sleep or we go for short walks. I'm not allowed to walk further than downstairs to the café. If my waters break, the cord could get trapped and he could die from oxygen starvation.

I've had so many visitors, and I feel so loved and so lucky.

I have been in the hospital for ten days so far, and I'm so fed up with nothing to do. I'm not used to sitting around doing nothing physical. I'm left with my thoughts, which since you died, are mostly about you, including the visions of you lying dead on the tracks.

Michael's bringing the dogs tonight so I can see them and so they know I'm ok. They are so excited to see me. I have snuck out into the car park to be with them for half an hour.

The dogs are staying at your house with John so Michael can go to work and then come straight over to see me.

Mary is a lady I met recently down at the yard where the horses are. She's one of those people who is like an open book. You know, she wears her heart on her sleeve. I trusted her quickly and told her about you. She's looking after the horses for me, no questions asked. Nor does she want any money for it. What a kind woman, Mum. You would have liked her.

It is the 20th of July 2018, and the doctor has decided to try and turn Ronnie so I can have him naturally. I am down in the labour suite. They scan me before the procedure and Ronnie has moved into the right position already without any help, so I've been induced. I feel such relief. He's on his way, and I couldn't be happier. I don't care about the physical pain, as long as he arrives safely.

I am moved back up to the ward to wait for the induction to work. It happens fairly quickly. I try everything to help him on his way. I bounce on the ball continually for a couple of hours, then I walk around the car park at speed for about an hour. It's nice to be out. I send Michael home for some rest, and I carry on bouncing. The contractions worsen, and I feel happy. I take a bath and they get more painful more quickly. I tell the midwife but something isn't right. They are too sharp and last too long. Nothing is happening other than constant contractions that don't stop. I'm breathing deeply a lot, and I feel dizzy now. I ring Michael and tell him to head over while they take me back down to the labour suite.

The midwives debate with each other if they should give me an injection to reverse the induction and send me back to the ward.

This thought makes me feel exhausted and sad. I thought I'd be on my way out of here soon with my baby boy, and ready to start a new life. I have got the machine hooked up, reading the contractions and Ronnie's heart rate. His heart is fluttering around and it worries me, but they don't seem too concerned. All of a sudden, his heart disappears so I try and shuffle the thing around to find it and I can't. It's gone. I feel panicked. I can't lose my boy. I casually call the midwife and she can't find it either. She tries for what seems like forever and her facial expression changes. She looks at us and says, 'I'm just going to find the doctor'. Michael can't cope with the thought so, he leaves and goes outside. I'm left sitting on this bed alone. My mind goes into meltdown as I decide my boy is dead.

The doctor brings in a scan machine. I stare at the screen and expect to see his still body with no sound to the heart. I hear the heart beating strongly and I see his moving body. I laugh with relief. Michael walks in and I look at him with a smile. He knows. The doctor looks at us and says, 'I'm sorry but he's now breech'. I don't care. He's alive! She tells us we can go straight down for a C-section. I'm so happy I could burst. Yes, thank you so much!

Mum, he's here, and he's so perfect. This tiny little person has filled my heart with love, hope, and such joy.

Michael is besotted with his little boy.

The C-section went well. What a strange experience though. He has dark brown hair and he weighs 7lbs 12oz. He's ten days early. He was born on the 21 July 2018.

When I got back to the ward at around 2 am, Michael went home, and I lay upright in shock that my Ronnie was finally here. I'm in awe of him, and the love I have for him is so strong. I don't sleep at all. I just lie there staring at him. He's so precious, and I can't quite believe he's mine.

I watch Michael sit and stare, holding his little hands for hours. I've waited for this moment, to watch that man with our child; our child who is warm, breathing, and full of life.

Chapter Ten

*T*hree months have passed, Mum. It's gone so quick. I still find myself staring at this beautiful being in disbelief that he's mine. He has given me the perfect reason to be happy, and I am, Mum.

He's a very calm and happy baby, Mum. You would love him.

I no longer picture you dead in pieces or stepping towards the train. I dream about you meeting Ronnie, and holding him in the way you held Olivia and Harry. Just loving every ounce of him.

I'm going to take Ronnie to Devon, and I will spread the remainder of your ashes with Jack's on that mountain where he rests. I know you would like it down there.

～

We have come to visit you at your grave; the place I've not been to for so long.

I've brought Ronnie to show you.

I stand at your grave, and I tell Ronnie about you.

I've brought a picture for you of him. I'll leave it at your head stone.

It's time to go now, Mum. I'll bring him back to see you again. We are going to meet Hayley and John for lunch.

We leave and I look down at Ronnie. He gives me the biggest smile his face can make. My heart melts.

About Me

I am 32. A young woman living in the East Midlands of England with her husband, Michael. I am a simple, happy, easily pleased kind of person. I don't expect much from people, as I have learnt to seek out what I want from my life and have a resilient nature. I can reach my many goals even though they take me a long time to achieve.

The life she, my mum, created for me was pretty full. I was given freedom, quite a lot of it, to go on adventures and learn from my own mistakes. She supported me but was also brutal in her honesty. She didn't like to sugarcoat the truth if it meant it would hurt me later on in life; she would rather I knew already.

I was an energetic, short-tempered red-headed child. I grew up not quite understanding how to control my behaviour, until I got my very first horse. I then became less intense, less short-tempered, and I became tired.

I was eleven when I decided I wanted to become a farrier; not many people believed in me but she did. She went above and beyond, organising extra time at school for maths and English, travelling with me to the open days at college and helping me write all my 200 handwritten letters to the potential training farriers. She gave me the option, and I grabbed it with both hands and never let it go. I wasn't given it all though. She brought us up in such a way that we always had options but the options included working hard and earning our own money to provide for ourselves. The cost of college was expensive and my family had to dig deep so I could go. I'll be eternally grateful to them all for that.

When I built up my own business she became my PA, and she was brilliant at it.

The passion I have for horses still strives on, and I improve my skills everyday.

Now, four years since she died, I am stronger, and I am more resilient then I ever thought I could be.

My love is urgent and constant, and I have found my place. I am happier than I have ever been.

I still speak to my therapist; not regularly anymore but he's always there when I need him.

I now suffer from anxiety. It quietly creeps in at times of stress but, over the years, I've learnt to recognise the signs, and I then ease the pressure I put on myself. It's constant but I am in control of it most of the time.

Printed in Great Britain
by Amazon